EXPLORE
the *transactions* between yourself and others . . .
those that contribute to self-fulfillment
and those that hinder growth.

DISCOVER
the psychological *games* that are played whenever
people come together . . . the games *you* play.

BECOME
the full, joyous, responsible, *loving*
Christian that God intended you to be.

Muriel M. James, a celebrated Christian
minister and one of the most widely-read
disciples of the late Dr. Eric Berne—
founder of transactional analysis—
combines her intimate knowledge of
psychology and the church to offer you
exciting, effective new ways to achieve
your most cherished human goals . . .

Bantam Books by Muriel M. James

BORN TO LOVE
THE OK BOSS

BORN TO LOVE

TRANSACTIONAL ANALYSIS IN THE CHURCH

MURIEL M. JAMES

BANTAM BOOKS
TORONTO · NEW YORK · LONDON · SYDNEY

BORN TO LOVE

*A Bantam Book / published by arrangement with
Addison-Wesley Publishing Co., Inc.*

PRINTING HISTORY

Addison-Wesley edition published August 1973

2nd printing ... November 1973	5th printing .... April 1975
3rd printing.... November 1974	6th printing .... May 1975
4th printing .... February 1975	7th printing .... April 1976

*Religion Book Club edition published June 1973
Bantam edition / June 1977
2nd printing ... July 1978
3rd printing ... June 1980
4th printing ... September 1981*

ISBN 0-553-20620-6

Published simultaneously in the United States and Canada

PRINTED IN THE UNITED STATES OF AMERICA

13 12 11 10 9 8 7 6 5 4

To Love
is to move
from death into Life

We have loved each other from the beginning,
and I give thanks for this joy—

to my children:
Gail Ann, Duncan, and John—

and my grandchildren:
Raymond, Bradley, Kathy, Julie, and Ian—

and my stepchildren:
Ernest, Lenora, Dianne, and Douglas—

and my step grandchildren:
Skye, Christiana, Kimberly, Sharon,
Daniella, Victoria—

and my foster children:
Diana, Jenny, Sherry, Karen, Julie,
Deanna, and Pam—

and my beloved husband, Ernest Brawley
who, with strength and tenderness,
loves all these children along with me.

Muriel James

PREFACE

This book is a result of my interest and training in theology and psychology. The intent of it is to show how the church and its people can be understood through the use of transactional analysis.

I care about the church. I care about it because as an institution it is concerned with people and relationships. It frequently fails in its mission, but the fact that it fails does not mean it is without value. I also care about the church because of the people in it. Many who are closest to me now I met in the church or as a direct result of its activity. I have been studying theology and psychology for about 20 years. Transactional analysis, one branch of psychology, is so practical that I want to show how it can be used to understand people in the church.

The title of my doctoral thesis in adult education at the University of California was *The Effect of National and International Crisis on the Development of Hebrew Adult Education from 1800 BC to 220 AD.* As I was teaching in the field of adult education I became excited when I started reading in the Talmud about the strong focus on adult education among the ancient Hebrews and how their educational views and practices were influenced by their history of captivity, freedom, and exile, and their interaction with countries such as Egypt, Babylonia, Assyria, Persia, Greece, and Rome.

I strongly believe that the ancient Hebrews' unique educational emphasis, which was always related to their theology, was one of the most important factors in their survival as a people. In fact, some of their educational principles, reflected in the Kallah and at their academy in the city of Sura, Babylonia (in 220 AD), became the framework on which I founded the

Laymen's School of Religion in 1959 in Berkeley, California.

At that time, aside from the occasional Bible class, very little was available in the churches in adult education, yet the hunger for theology was high. The Laymen's School of Religion helped fill this hunger as an interdenominational, interfaith school for adults. The School did not have a building or adequate office equipment; like a university extension it borrowed space from others and put on classes throughout the San Francisco Bay area. It grew rapidly, and over 10,000 people of widely differing backgrounds and theological beliefs studied in the school during the next ten years. The faculty members were academic scholars with the rare ability to communicate difficult subjects in understandable ways and without bias.

Gradually the interests of the adult students and the staff, like that of much of society, changed focus. From a direct interest in theology, *per se*, the interest of some members widened to the application of theological beliefs, and the interests of others shifted to a humanistic concern. The fields of psychology and education became crucial tools for understanding contemporary living.

In 1970 property for the Laymen's School was secured in Lafayette, California. It was named the Oasis Center, and new programs were added to the existing ones of the School.

One of the programs is an "extended" family which is a new form of the church. This group of some twenty families study and play together, give each other emotional support, and are of service to the community. As Oasis Associates they belong to different churches and, in some cases, to no church at all, yet each one brings uniqueness and love to the group.

Other new programs at the Oasis include: community education for the general public; clinical training for mental health professionals, clergy, and teachers; management training for businesses and government personnel; a day school with a therapeutic dimension for teenagers; and a residential program for foster children. Transactional Analysis is the basic method used in all programs.

The future is open. New needs and interests will emerge. Hopefully, I will design new programs in response to the needs; hopefully the programs will show forth love.

I think of love as unconditional goodwill toward other people. I believe love happens because of the *Love* that once was, still is, and always will be.

It is impossible to thank all of those who have taught, befriended, guided, and studied with me in churches, universities, hospitals, schools and therapeutic situations, but to a few, I must speak my gratitude.

To Dr. Eric Berne, to the International Transactional Analysis Association, the Transactional Analysis Institute of Contra Costa County (in Lafayette, California), and even more important, to my clients, who helped me develop therapeutic knowledge and skills, thank you.

To Reverend Dale Cooper and the Montclair Presbyterian Church, Oakland, California, who first introduced and loved me into the Christian faith, thank you. To the Reverend Dr. Chauncy Bloom and the Orinda Community Church, Orinda, California, where I was ordained a Congregational minister, and to the Reverend Dr. Richard Norberg, Conference Minister of the United Church of Christ, who first invited me to serve communion, thank you. To Dr. Hans Reudi-Weber who so kindly asked me to teach and lead worship for the World Council of Churches in Bossey, Switzerland, thank you. I believe I became a citizen of the world during that experience.

I also wish to thank the theological professors, denominational officials, and dedicated laymen and women who worked with me to found and administer the Laymen's School of Religion—in particular, Paul Ehret, Robert Leslie, Jean and Sherman Johnson, Charles McCoy, John Turpin, Victoria Harding, Margaretta and James Jeffery, Harley Spitler, Shirley Brown, Maria Smith, Victor Gold, Harland Hogue, Don Masse, Arnold Come, Theodore Gill, Neil Hamilton, Robert Rodenmayer, C. Clifford Crummy, John

Hadsell, Trevor Hoy, Don Falkenberg, Edward Setchko, and Harold Farzee.

To Maria Smith, Marilyn Borton, Norma Webster, and Jessie Budd, who typed and retyped and re-retyped this manuscript, thank you.

To Teresa Mary Dolan, Virginia Blacklidge, Allyn Bradford, Robert Chartier, Victoria Harding, Norma James, George Torney, Carl Zeigler, Betsy and Howard Friend, Jr., Mary Lou Jacoby, Arthur C. Beck, Jr., and Mary Stephens, who read all or part of the manuscript and made many valuable suggestions, my sincere gratitude.

To those who contributed photographs used in this book—Betty Jean Boone (page 21), Daniel Buop (page 139), Ron Ching (pages 13, 21, 138, 152), Norma James (page 149), Walter Lau (pages 46–47), Lynne Miller (pages 28–29), and John Pearson (page 217)—to all my warm thanks and appreciation.

And to John James, my son and professional colleague at the Oasis, who took the rest of the very fine photographs, again my loving thanks.

February 1973   M.J.
Lafayette, California

NOTES TO THE
GROUP LEADER

This book can be used by one person who is studying alone or it can be used by a group, with each person having a copy. If you are the group leader, then you are the kind of person who cares about others. The notes following are caring suggestions for you to use.

The exercises in relevancy that follow each chapter (beginning at Chapter 2) are intended to show how the theory, encompassed in the events at First Church, can be applied by the reader to his own situation.

Some exercises are listed for individual use, some for group use. Many of them are interchangeable. It is not necessary to use them all. If time is limited, use those that seem most pertinent to your situation.

When using the book in a group, it is helpful if the group members will read ahead. Each chapter could be summarized by different people as the course progresses. Others could comment on the sections that interest them the most. Small committees of two or three persons could suggest the most relevant exercises for group use.

There are two basic ways to influence others, by the use of propaganda or by the use of education. Some parents, teachers, and churches are propagandists and arbitrarily impose their own opinions and attitudes on others. Other parents, teachers, and churches are educators and do not try to compel or coerce people. Instead they offer other possibilities by providing a setting in which people can think and act in freedom. Freedom is not the opposite of compulsion, nor is it license, nor an end in itself. No.

Freedom is a springboard or a footbridge to communion. Everyone has a creative instinct to move out, shape materials, make speech, tools, programs, etc. Each person also has an instinct for communion. In a loving community both instincts are given freedom to develop. Hopefully this book will increase people's freedom to use their creative potentials and bring into communion those who study together. Please don't impose or compel—simply offer.

Note: Additional publications of transactional analysis are listed in the back of this book. In particular, *Born to Win: Transactional Analysis with Gestalt Experiments*, and *Winning with People: Group Exercises in Transactional Analysis* (co-authored by Muriel James and Dorothy Jongeward, published by Addison Wesley, Reading, Mass.), would be most helpful as extra resource texts.

CONTENTS

3
YOU CAN
UNDERSTAND PERSONALITY

4
YOU CAN
ANALYZE TRANSACTIONS

5
YOU CAN SEE
GAMES PEOPLE PLAY

6

YOU CAN REWRITE
A PSYCHOLOGICAL SCRIPT

7
YOU CAN FIND
MEANING IN TIME

8
EPILOGUE:
A TRANSACTIONAL THEOLOGY

BORN
TO LOVE

"Ask, and it shall be given you; seek, and ye shall find; knock, and it shall be opened unto you," but trespass, and you may be banned.

Forgive us and our churches our trespasses: for turning away people, for turning people away from us.
Let us open wide our doors and show forth the *Love* that was, is, and ever shall be. We ask this in the strong name of Jesus Christ, Lord and Savior, who continually reveals the meaning and action of love.
Amen, Amen

YOU ARE INVITED ...
WITH LOVE

Perhaps you have wondered from time to time about who you are and where you are going, about how and why you are in the church, about how the church sometimes contributes positively to your life and how it sometimes fails to meet your needs. Perhaps you have also wondered why people in the church respond to each other as they do, either positively or negatively; why some people remain active and enthused over the church and some people lose interest, become discontented, or rebellious toward it.

If you are looking for a tool to use for understanding yourself, if you are looking for a way to understand how and why people get involved with each other, this book is for you. It will answer many of your questions related to individual people and their personalities. It will also answer many of your questions related to what goes on between two persons. Furthermore, it will answer some questions related to the dynamics of various groups in the church.

Each one of us hopes for love, at least, understanding and acceptance as we spend part of our lives in different groups: family groups, on-the-job groups, social groups, and church groups. This book may be used to advantage by an individual or any type of group, but is specifically designed for church groups and people who go to church or are thinking of going.

Some church groups function smoothly, get the job done, and leave their members with positive feelings. Most people hope for, even search for, groups like this. The climate of such groups is one in which faith, hope, and love are experienced, not just talked about. The overall atmosphere and the tone of such groups are rewarding to their members. Problems are approached constructively. Feelings are expressed honestly.

Other church groups seem to be almost destructive or, to say the least, dissatisfying. They leave the group members feeling frustrated, and with a sense that something important is missing. The "something important" that is missing is understanding, tolerance, and love. Instead there are crosscurrents of negative feelings and sudden unpredictable responses that break down group cohesion and cause painful feelings of mistrust and resentment.

Another type of church group most people try to avoid is one in which the members are unable to come to satisfying conclusions. Meetings go on and on but important decisions are not made. Small details are focused on instead of the main issues. Boredom and frustration are experienced.

The thoughtful person puzzles over the difference between the constructive groups he would like to go back to because they are lively and life-giving, and the destructive or going-nowhere groups from which he turns away, dissatisfied because they are deadening.*

A TOOL FOR UNDERSTANDING

One way of understanding people as individuals and as part of a group is through the principles of transactional analysis. Transactional analysis is both a psychological theory and a psychological method. It was developed by the psychiatrist Dr. Eric Berne (1910–1970), author of a number of books on the subject, including the well-known *Games People Play*.

Dr. Berne, a graduate of McGill University, entered professional life as a community physician. Later he became a psychiatrist in private practice, then joined the Army Medical Corps. He served as a consultant and lecturer to numerous universities, hospitals, and clinics, and selected Erik Erikson as his own analyst. When Dr. Berne returned to private practice after

* "He" refers to persons of either sex except where "she" is definitely applicable.

the war he put particular emphasis on group therapy and broke away from traditional psychoanalytical theory to develop his own method, which he called "Transactional Analysis."[1]

One of Dr. Berne's first papers on this new concept, "Ego States in Psychotherapy," published in 1957, influenced some of its readers to study the subject further. To meet this interest, clinical seminars were held every week in Carmel and in San Francisco. Professionals, excited by Dr. Berne's ideas, met with him regularly, tested and elaborated on the theory, loved him, and wept for him and for themselves when he died.

In 1958, when I was doing post-graduate work in pastoral counseling at Pacific School of Religion, one of my supervisors was Kenneth Everts, M.D., currently president of the International Transactional Analysis Association. He showed me an early paper of Eric's and invited me to attend the seminars in San Francisco. This I did gratefully and thus began my relationship with Eric Berne, who became my teacher, clinical supervisor, and friend—and who remained so until his death, twelve years later.

This relationship was important to me for several reasons, not the least of which was that when I had learned the theory he proposed, I could apply it to my other academic interests: theology, sociology, philosophy, and education.

Originally transactional analysis was for use in group therapy, where people needed help in straightening out the problems in their lives. From this original use, transactional analysis (often abbreviated to TA) has been applied to a rapidly increasing number of situations. Currently it is also used as a training tool in government agencies, business and industry, community action groups, hospitals, correctional institutions, schools, and now in the church and church related groups.

The methods used in TA are based on the premise that anyone can learn to understand himself, understand other people in his life, and understand how to improve his interpersonal relations.

READING AND STUDY PLAN

The following chapters of this book present the theory of Transactional Analysis and show how it can be applied. Both theory and examples are woven into the fabric of events going on at First Church, where Tom Hardy is the pastor, Joe Miles his assistant, Mr. Pennyworth the treasurer, Mrs. Pillar, chairman of the women's society, and Mr. Tenor is choir director.

These and others portrayed in vignette form are composites of many people I have known and loved. The situations described are disguised and, although based on fact, do not refer to events in any specific church.

Each chapter presents one or more episodes in the life of First Church. The events described and analyzed in this somewhat typical parish take place between a Thursday evening pot-luck supper and a Friday midnight. The intent is to show what can happen in the life of a church in a short period of about thirty hours and how transactional analysis can be used to understand these events. To more clearly distinguish between these two elements, *this typeface will be used in describing the events in the church* and this typeface will be used in presenting and discussing basic TA theory.

Persons who read this for individual use or for use in study groups will be able to draw parallels between their own experiences and those described. A TA goal at the end of each chapter summarizes the material in the context of Love.

Also at the end of each chapter is a study section (beginning with Chapter 2), titled *Exercises in Relevancy*. The individual reader may use these sections to become more aware of himself; study groups may use them to gain insight into church problems and how they can be solved. Some of these exercises are labeled for individual use; some for group study. Many of them can be used in both ways.

The book is organized so that the material could be covered by a group in eight to twelve weeks. However, many will want to take a longer period because one insight leads to another, which is one reason why TA is stimulating, exciting, and rewarding. Transactional analysis can actually make a significant difference in a person's life and in the life of the church.

For some it may be a little like having been blind and suddenly being able to see, like having been hungry and suddenly being fed—or like having been in prison and suddenly made free.

MAKING A CONTRACT

When TA is used in counseling, one of the most important steps is the formation of a contract between the client and the counselor. The contract is always specific. It focuses around solving problems, changing attitudes and behavior, or alleviating physical distress. To establish a contract the therapist asks a question such as "What are you here to see me for?" or "What do you want to be cured of?" or "What about yourself would you like to change?"

The client, if not avoiding the issue, will respond with a statement such as "I want to get over my depression," or "I'm here because my husband wants to leave me and I need to understand why," or "I want to get up the courage to change jobs," or "I need to stop getting so angry with my children."

If the statement reveals a decision to do something about a particular problem or clearly defines a goal, and if the problem has the potential for being solved or the goal can be reached, both client and therapist agree that this is a contract. In the process of therapy a person may make a succession of contracts; some can be fulfilled rapidly, some take longer. These contracts lead a person to a deep sense of freedom and the recognition that he was born to be loved and born to be loving.

If you wish to increase your awareness of love and your potential for loving you can make contracts with yourself as you read this book and experiment with the exercises at the end of each chapter.

One possible contract would be to read each chapter and work through the exercises in relevancy that apply to you. Another would be to form a study group for the same purpose. This would require selection of a leader and commitment by the participants for a minimum of eight sessions.

A third contract might be to listen openly and nonjudgmentally in all group discussions for one month and to give back straight information to the group about your own feelings and thoughts. A fourth possibility would be to keep a diary of the insights you suddenly have as you read along and of the ideas you may wish to explore further.

A fifth, and more important contract, would be to evaluate and increase your love quotient. As everyone knows who has experienced it even briefly, love is a many splendored thing. According to Pitirim Sorokin,[2] human love has five dimensions: intensity, extensity, duration, purity, and adequacy. A person's ability to love in each of these dimensions can be roughly measured from zero to one hundred percent. Each dimension has extremes, for example:

The *intensity* of love is less when performing a courteous act than when risking one's life for someone. The first might be given 5 points, the second 90 points.

The *extensity* of love is also roughly measurable from the extreme of love only of one's self or family to that of love of all mankind.

The *duration* of love may be momentary, as when a soldier briefly risks his life for a comrade and later becomes disinterested, or it may be a life-long commitment that one person makes to another, such as in some marriages or life-long friendships.

The *purity* of love at its highest level is without exploitation, but if love is merely a means to an end, the purity is close to zero.

The *adequacy* of love can also be measured. Many parents who love their children parent them unwisely and the children become spoiled, irresponsible, or dishonest. In such cases the aim of love does not bring the hoped-for consequences of love. Others may not love their children but still get satisfying results. In both cases the love is inadequate. When the subjective goal and objective consequences of love are identical or compatible, the love is truly adequate.

Love is an energy. It is a creative healing force. It is also self-perpetuating if people develop a reservoir of love by "tuning in" to God, who is *Love*. Unfortunately, people do not know how to tune in very efficiently. Time, effort, and money have been spent to understand and harness various physical energies. Now the generation of love-energy needs attention. More individuals, families, and churches need to produce love in abundance so that, like other forms of energy, it can be stored, yet used continually and flow spontaneously. Love begets love.

Churches have always proclaimed the gospel of love. They have even enacted the gospel of love. But it has not been enough. Each person needs to make contracts to increase his or her loving kindness in all five dimensions.

Some people find it hard to commit themselves to a contract because they have had poor experiences with people using psychology, some because of a sense of personal inadequacy or a fear of discovering something unpleasant. Still others may have an attitude of superiority and claim that psychology is not necessary. "All you need is faith," they may say. "If you just believe hard enough everything will be solved."

However, the flick of a TV dial inevitably brings people and their psychological problems into your awareness. The flip of magazine or newspaper pages does the same. The ring of the doorbell or phone may be the signal of a friend in trouble. Your ability to love, reinforced by a sound, healthy understanding of people, can be a redeeming force wherever you are.

Unfortunately, some people who believe in the religious dimension of life and in the importance of the Church seem unwilling to consider new ideas and methods for understanding human behavior. Many others *are* willing, concerned, even eager to understand the dynamics of what happens between people. I hope you are one of these and willing to read on. This book explains a new form of ancient and basic truth, and my hope is that you will experience it like a well-spring of new life, at your inner core of being.

Birth is one experience we have in common. Death is another. Between those two events is what some people have called *Life*, what others have called living, still others have defined as existence, as living death, or as that which is worse than death itself.

To feel half dead when life calls is a tragedy. To feel angry or sad for being born is heartbreaking. To feel dismayed or hopeless when the sun rises or sets is a waste of the *Love* that was given "in the beginning."

But so it is for some people. They wait and wait— often for a magical something that will never come. They deny themselves *Life*, with its joy and warmth, its laughter and pain, its loneliness and grief. They deny the presence of the here and now, forgetting that the here and now is what they are given to live in.

INVITATION TO DISCOVERY

This, then, is an invitation to read, to think, to discover. If you accept the invitation you will become more aware of your individual personality structure. You will learn why you think, feel, and do the things that you do. You will understand why you are drawn toward certain persons, sometimes at the first glance —and, perhaps, why you turn away from or try to avoid others.

You will also learn about *transactions* between people—how to identify the transactions that contribute to growth and those that hinder growth. You will learn some of the psychological *games* that are played whenever people come together and how all people sometimes act on the basis of their subconscious life *script*. Through learning these things, you will discover more of your own uniqueness and the unlimited potentials you already have for self-realization and love.

YOU CAN USE TRANSACTIONAL ANALYSIS

MIXED FEELINGS
AT THE POTLUCK SUPPER

Hurried footsteps sounded on the cement path below the window of Pastor Hardy's study, disturbing his thoughts early this Friday morning. He had been pacing the floor, going over the events of the previous evening, looking for the threads of discord that had permeated the church potluck supper. It was too early for Myra, his secretary, to come to work. Could it be someone who wanted to talk about last night? Mrs. Pillar perhaps?

The supper had been well attended. It was the last event before summer vacations, a kind of "winding up" of the church school year. Mrs. Pillar had seen to it in her usual capable way that one of the women's circles had made the decorations. The red and white checkered table cloths and white shasta daisies provided an inviting atmosphere in the multipurpose hall.

Even some men, who normally didn't attend the monthly potlucks, looked around the room with approval as they entered. Maybe it was the odor of good food that made them smile in anticipation. After all, the women of the church were good cooks, and the hot dishes smelled even better than usual.

Tom Hardy remembered that as he walked into the hall he had been humming an old gospel hymn that was a favorite from his childhood prayer meeting days, "Work for the Night is Coming." At the door he had met Austin Tenor, choir leader at First Church

*for the past twelve years. Softly harmonizing a few
bars of the hymn the two had entered the room together. Tom's niece, Kathy, and his nephew, Raymond, smiled brightly at him as they entered, and
his wife, who had come down early to help out, waved
to him.*

*Over at one side of the room two well-liked young
couples who sponsored the junior high group were
talking enthusiastically to a small group of 12- or
13-year-olds. They were making plans to canvass the
neighborhood, to speak to families about pollution,
and to suggest ways in which the families might get
involved in trying to solve local problems. Tom
Hardy's son, John, was with the group and obviously
enjoying himself. Tom suspected that although John
had a definite interest in the subject of pollution,
Mr. Tenor's niece, Norma, was an extra reason for
his enthusiasm.*

*Herbert Vague looked much less enthusiastic. As
he arrived with his mother and his wife June, he
looked pinched, sallow, and slightly cowed. June's
face was haggard, her eyes guarded, as she guided her
mother-in-law to a seat in the corner. As usual,
Grandma Vague had a scattered, flighty, and somewhat disoriented appearance about her.*

*Recently she had had a series of small strokes
which had left her forgetful and slightly confused.
June had complained to Tom Hardy, "I'm so tired of
Grandma pattering up and down the hall in those
sloppy slippers! I just know she listens at our bedroom
door after we go to bed at night. Furthermore, when
Herbert's at work she hangs around me all the time
and if I don't talk to her every minute she wanders
out the door and down the street. Honestly, I just
can't take any more."*

*As Pastor Hardy saw them enter he thought
"There's a family that really needs help, but I wonder
how to get them to accept it. Well, at least they're
here tonight so that's a good sign."*

*The four-year-old Roger twins, looking angelic as
usual, were nudging and kicking each other under*

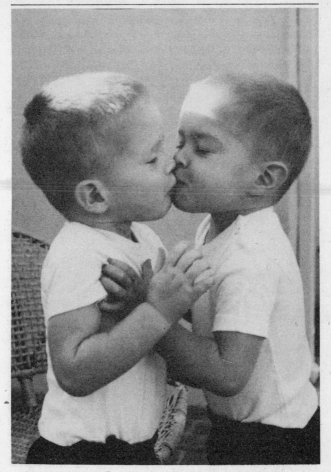

Intimacy between identical twins is common because of their identical genetic heritage and prenatal environment. Even if separated for years, identical twins, often unknowingly, respond to what goes on in each other. They may each experience depression, illness, joy, etc. at the same time the other experiences it. One of the reasons people attend church is in the hope of finding intimacy and love.

one of the tables. Their older sister was trying to placate them while their mother, Lisa Roger, a petite brunette, moved around the room glancing at the men who were there but pretending not to be doing so.

Lisa was a member of the choir, had a fine voice, and often sang solos during Sunday morning service. However, even when she wasn't in the star soloist role, there was something about her walk and the way she crossed her legs and batted her eyes that gave people the impression she expected to be applauded as though on stage. Sometimes she got the recognition she was seeking; sometimes she didn't.

Only last month Tom Hardy had walked into a room unexpectedly where two men were discussing Lisa in quite unflattering terms. They accused her of playing the psychological seductive game called Rapo. As one described the game, "She gives men the come-on, but if they act interested she brushes them off self-righteously, acting as if they had tried to rape her."

However, this evening those at the dinner were so accustomed to Lisa's ways, to the peculiarities of the Vague family, and to the boisterousness of the Roger twins that they watched them indulgently rather than critically.

In the center of the room was the Birthday Table. It had been a well-established custom that anyone who had had a birthday since the last church supper, or who would have a birthday before the month was out, was eligible to be remembered with a surprise birthday cake, complete with candles and the recipient's name in icing. Each celebrant had the chance to blow out his own candles and become the center of attention while everyone sang "Happy Birthday" in his honor. When a small child had his turn at the Birthday Table, he often bragged a little about how old he was getting to be. If the turn fell to a grownup who said "Let's not talk about age. It's too depressing," he was kidded but permitted to keep his subterfuge.

Mr. Pennyworth, the church treasurer, had looked

BIRTHDAYS ARE FOR JOY

One may experience a childlike sense of joy
during a birthday celebration. Some people think
birthday parties are silly or only for children; others
experience gloom as the result of some earlier birthday
that was unhappy. Yet the celebration of Christmas
and any other birthday is a time for happiness.

*at the table while trying to appear casual. A smile
had come to his face. Evidently he was remembered
with his name on one of the cakes. Bob, a teenager,
had looked at the table then turned around abruptly
and walked over towards Sally, the Senior High
moderator. Some of the younger children who looked
at the cake did so with glowing eyes and, thought
Pastor Hardy, were probably trying to figure out how
to manipulate the scene to get the biggest piece with
the most frosting. Myra, the church secretary, looked
a little downcast, perhaps recalling her childhood
birthdays which were only recognized by her parents
several days after they occurred. But on the whole,
the evening had started out pretty well.*

*Looking back on it, the pastor puzzled over what
might have caused the tension just when everything
seemed pleasant. Was it the eight or ten teenagers
who came in after everyone had already started eating? He remembered their good-natured noise, their
laughing and joking as all eyes turned in their direction. They were hungry and happy, barefoot with
faded jeans, knit shirts and sleeveless tops, the kind
of near-uniform that many high school young people
wore. Three of the boys had stacked their guitars in
the corner before joining the others at the table. All
had heaped their plates high, signaling their good
spirits and healthy appetites.*

*Pastor Hardy remembered that Mr. Tenor, the choir
director, had smiled good-naturedly at the guitars,
but that Mrs. Pillar's back had stiffened at the smell
of the cigarette smoke and the sight of jeans and long
shaggy hair. As the evening progressed, others from
Mrs. Pillar's circle, though busy in the kitchen, began
to throw disapproving glances at the teenagers while
whispering between themselves.*

*Why, Pastor Hardy mused, were the women in the
kitchen upset? The young people had done nothing
wrong. Far from it. They had merely assumed they
were welcome no matter how they looked or how much
they ate.*

Dessert was scarcely finished when Joe Miles, youth

minister for the past year, introduced these late comers as a new folk song group he had helped to organize. They were here, he announced, to perform some of their own selections.

Even now, sitting in his study the following morning, Pastor Hardy heard once more the haunting, catchy melodies of the folk music which had been sung with deep pathos. The program had indeed been different from those given at the usual monthly church potluck supper—a refreshing change.

Footsteps coming up the stairs broke his train of thought once more. The outside office door slammed. Another opened, and there stood Mrs. Pillar herself with a frown on her face and a hand on her hip. Taking a deep breath she plunged in.

"I'm fed up. For years I've helped out in this church in all kinds of ways but I never saw such a display of bad manners as I did last night at that supper! What's the matter with Joe? Why isn't he doing a better job with our kids? That was an arty-party kind of show going on last night! Jeans! Long hair! Guitars! Bongo drums! Smoking! In our church!

"And furthermore," she exploded, "what happened to you, of all people? You're supposed to be the pastor around here! After all the work that we in the Mayflower Circle went to, making those decorations and planning those hot dishes and salads and desserts, you never even acknowledged our efforts! Those kids ran the show last night. No one else had a chance, much less any thanks for all the work. And look how hard we tried!"

Bottled up tensions were now out in the open. Various feelings had started to surface the previous evening but right now Mrs. Pillar's anger was really erupting. She claimed she wanted to do the right thing for everyone, including the young people. But as the new and unexpected events had taken place, her warm feelings toward youth had changed to feelings of annoyance, resentment, and even jealousy at being ignored.

Pastor Hardy, at that moment, had the opportunity

Styles of music and use of
leisure time may cause
conflict between young
people and their elders.

*for an impromptu counseling session. Right then,
without any further delay, was the time to help Mrs.
Pillar sort out her feelings, to help her gain some
insight into what had happened the previous night
that upset her so drastically.*

*"Sit down, Jean," he said, "I'm glad you came in to
talk about last night. I can see you're feeling pretty
strongly about what happened at the potluck. Go on,
please."*

*So it happened, on this particular Friday morning,
that Pastor Hardy introduced Transactional Analysis
to Mrs. Pillar as a way of understanding what had
happened and why she felt the way she did.*

TRANSACTIONAL ANALYSIS
FOR UNDERSTANDING PEOPLE

From time to time every pastor faces problems
with his parishioners. Parishioners also have problems
with their pastors. Therefore, everyone needs help.
The theory and method of Transactional Analysis can
provide some of that help. Transactional analysis, as
developed by Dr. Eric Berne, is a psychological tool
which can be used by anyone to help them understand people and the ways people interact—both
positively and negatively—with each other.

According to Dr. Berne, his theory began to unfold
as he observed that behavioral changes took place in
his patients whenever a new stimulus (i.e., odor,
touch, sound, etc.), came into their environment.
These changes involved facial expressions, voice in-
flections, gestures, words, and sentence structure.[1]
It was as though there were several people inside a
single person. At various times any one of these
several persons seemed to be in control of the entire
personality.

Dr. Berne also observed that these various selves
transacted (interacted) in various ways with the
selves of other people and that these transactions
could be studied or analyzed. Sometimes the transactions had a hidden motive or agenda and lured
other persons into psychological *games*. Berne also
noted that people performed in ways that seemed

predetermined, often acting as though on stage and reading from a *script*. From these observations he developed his unique theory of Transactional Analysis —the analysis of people, and the exchanges which take place whenever human beings meet.

There are four phases to transactional analysis, and each will be discussed in detail in subsequent chapters. Briefly they are defined as follows:

Structural analysis: the analysis of individual personality.

Transactional analysis: the analysis of how people interact with one another.

Game analysis: the analysis of a series of transactions with an ulterior purpose leading to a *payoff*.

Script analysis: the analysis of life dramas that are consciously or subconsciously acted out.

WHAT MAKES TA UNUSUAL?

When Pastor Tom Hardy began to explain TA to Jean Pillar he first told her, "Jean, the vocabulary in TA is simple and straightforward. It can be readily understood. The few words needed to understand the theory are common to everyday living. These basic words are Parent, Adult, Child, transactions, games, and script.

"Of course, transactional analysis, as practiced by psychiatrists and other professionals, is based on sound psychological research, but that does not mean that you must have an academic understanding of psychology, sociology, or any of the other social sciences to benefit from its uses. In fact, some of the people who come to talk with me have less than a high school education. This doesn't keep them from learning and applying transactional analysis to their everyday problems."

Unlike some psychological systems which are understood and used only by professional psychotherapists, transactional analysis can be understood and used by everyone. It furthermore protects the dignity *of the individual because it encourages people to make their own contracts for change.*

Pastor Hardy frequently noticed that a counselee, searching for a way out of his tangled problems, experienced an immediate sense of relief with transactional analysis. He had once been told by a very desperate man that learning TA gave him a sense of power to cope with the immediate problems in his life and a feeling of hope that he would be able to find successful solutions to his problems.

THE MANY USES OF TA IN THE LOCAL CHURCH

One practical use of TA in the church is in pastoral counseling. In such a situation it frequently can be introduced in the last fifteen minutes of the first counseling session.[2] TA can also be used to understand any encounter between persons, such as that between Pastor Hardy and Jean Pillar—especially when the situation calls for the airing, understanding, and resolving of tensions.

Some other personal situations in which TA can be used are: when comforting someone in distress, when formulating realistic procedures, when discussing theological concepts, when helping someone recover a sense of joy, or when laughing, loving, or even lounging about with one person or in groups.

In a group situation it can be used for understanding the church staff or the dynamics of a congregational meeting. It can be used in groups to solve specific problems, such as how to raise funds, how to encourage attendance, and how to enlist church school teachers. It is also effective when evaluating church policies and programs for the purpose of estimating possible future failures as well as possible successes.

Transactional analysis can be used in committee work. For example, the finance committee at First Church often had difficulty in getting the approval of Mr. Pennyworth, the church treasurer, for an increase in the budget. He frequently growled, "Where is the money for *this* coming from, I'd like to know."

Some church school teachers are creative;
they encourage creativity, recognize the curiosity
of children, and know that loving one another
means learning how to care for all creation.

His critical and restrictive position on the expenditure of money was often at odds with the positions of other members of the committee.

Anne Green, the representative from the Church School on the committee, often responded to his growls with unrealistic suggestions, such as "Maybe pastor wouldn't mind if he waited a little while for his salary this month." This kind of comment made Mr. Pennyworth even more determined in his ways.

In such a situation, a chairman with an awareness of personality structure and a knowledge that each person is unique because of his different inherited capacities and different experiences may be able to encourage committee members to discuss money questions on the basis of fact, rather than on the basis of penny-pinching or impulsive spending.

Like many people, Anne Green responded to different situations and people in different ways. Although she was not an effective finance committee member, she was a good member of the Religious Education Board because she understood children and what they needed in the way of teachers. She recognized that not all teachers are competent; that some teach primarily from a sense of duty with little interest or energy to spend on preparation or follow-through. Yet, in spite of this, she often led teacher training sessions that caused indifferent teachers to become enthusiastically involved. To do this, she applied the principle of transacting openly and directly with her teachers, rather than covertly and with a hidden agenda.

The many problems of the choir—what music to choose, when to rehearse, how to recruit or "dismiss" old members, and how to recognize each person's talents—all can be considered and eased with a working knowledge of transactional analysis. For example, in First Church some of the older parishioners liked gospel songs such as "The Old Rugged Cross." Some of the young people liked "Blowin' in the Wind." Still others preferred the traditional majesty of Handel and Bach. Those who preferred one kind of music frequently criticized the others: "It's too old fashioned," or "I just can't get used to this new music. It's not church to me" or "Wow! who listens to that stuff any more?"

One thing Mr. Tenor, the choir director, needed to realize was that various music forms could be used in the church to meet different interests. Another was that the congregation needed to become aware of the values of each kind of music so all kinds could be tolerated and individuals could stop being critical of those who had different preferences.

Other church-related organizations—such as the Men's Club, Women's Society, adult study classes, and the youth groups—are more likely to work together with better understanding when they are aware of how transactional analysis can improve their unique interpersonal relations.

TA AND DENOMINATIONAL COMMITTEES

Those who work on denominational committees can use transactional analysis in much the same way as in the local church, to understand themselves and others and consequently be more effective.

Gary Jones was an eager young minister recently called to the pastorate of Terrace Church. He was excited at being asked to serve on the social action committee of the denomination but at the meetings often acted as though he were on stage, like a child trying to impress his elders.

Sam Morrison, a denominational executive, sometimes found his effectiveness was limited. In contrast to Gary, he acted like a parent toward others. He irritated committee members under the guise of trying to help them. They accused him of being dictatorial with his instructions and suggestions and of ignoring their personal feelings.

One night, after an unsuccessful meeting, Sam phoned Tom Hardy and asked for an honest opinion. Tom, in a non-judgmental tone of voice, responded, "I think, Sam, if you'll be more aware of how you act in the committee like a big parent, you could learn to control your judgmental tone of voice and that habit of yours of shaking your finger at people. Sometimes people who have a position of authority on a job turn off their childlike capacity to laugh and have fun. You don't need to be that way, Sam. Relax a little!"

Sam was able to say, "Tom, I guess you're right. Sometimes I talk down to people, just like my father did to me. I guess I should stop doing it."

To Gary, who phoned to complain about Sam after the same meeting, Tom suggested, "Gary, you've got a good mind and we need to listen to what you have to say, but sometimes when you clown around, when you laugh and joke at something serious that's being said, you turn people off. We all perform for each other from time to time, often on the basis of our psychological script. We act our parts, then wait for applause or boos. Next time a course in Transactional Analysis is given around here, why don't you take it? I took a course and it helped me to see myself a little more clearly. I don't always like what I see, but it's useful anyway."

INTERFAITH RELATIONS AND TA

Most interfaith committees meet infrequently, with a fluctuating attendance. Here, too, the concepts of transactional analysis can be used either by the committee as a whole, or by one individual who wants to understand how the dynamics of the group affect the decisions.

For example, the last time Tom Hardy met with the interfaith council, comprised of Catholic, Protestant, and Jewish representatives, he made several observations as the result of his TA training.

Dr. Goodman, the Methodist bishop, often got into the conversation like an over-nurturing parent. "Maybe his image of himself is that of being a good shepherd to all people," thought Tom Hardy. "He doesn't like any arguing and often tries to quiet our differences of opinion."

On the other hand, Tom noticed that Rabbi Cohen

did not avoid conflict and could be counted on to collect facts and evaluate the situation. His way of thinking objectively contributed to making sound inter-faith decisions. The Rabbi was a rational, thinking adult.

Father O'Malley of St. Luke's had still another style. If an air of tension seemed to be building up in the meeting, he would often come through with a goodnatured joke. He joshed with people as one youngster might with another.

These ways of behaving with people—as a nurturing parent, as a clear thinking adult, and as a fun-loving child—are some of the categories used in transactional analysis to explain who people are and why they behave as they do.

FURTHER CONSIDERATION OF
TA IN THE CHURCH

The transactional analyst under whom Tom Hardy had taken his initial training cautioned against an over-optimistic assumption that the knowledge of transactional analysis would erase all problems in the church. The use of transactional analysis or any other psychological method does not solve all personal issues, committee tensions, theological disputes, or concerns of church budget and church attendance. However, all problems can be analyzed through its use. When this is done the problems become understandable and therefore more likely to be solved.

In addition to its obvious use with seminary students and groups of clergy, TA can be taught and applied in a local church in several ways: (1) in sermons or a series of lectures followed by questions and answers, (2) in a study group using discussion methods and hopefully led by someone skilled in group process, and (3) in personal growth or counseling groups.

The International Transactional Analysis Association, Berkeley, California, accredits qualified TA instructors and therapists throughout the world. In a case where a nonaccredited instructor is used it is important that he is informed on TA, is respected by the group, and is aware of his own strengths and weaknesses in group leadership. A study group leader needs to have many of the skills a good therapist has and be willing to respect the privacy of others and deal gently with their dreams.

All leaders of personal growth and counseling groups need to be sharply aware of the important differences between TA counseling groups whose members meet primarily for counseling and TA study groups whose members meet to study, but also interact outside the group, either in the total life of the church, or in social or vocational situations.

The reason for this caution is that transactional analysis was originally developed by Dr. Eric Berne as a treatment method for psychotherapists to use in treating patients within a group structure, either in a hospital or in a private practice. In both situations patients have some measure of privacy. Neither their last names, addresses, nor place of work are mentioned in the group.

This privacy is not natural within a church structure. Therefore, if a pastor or other professional has a TA group and focuses on the treatment of psychological problems, he needs to insist that everything of a personal nature discussed in the group be kept completely confidential. It is absolutely essential that whatever is disclosed to group members is not made public.

Some persons feel that they must "report" everything to a spouse, a relation, or a friend. Unless such persons are willing to make a commitment of confidentiality, they should not be included in a church TA group. Nor should they be included if their personalities indicate an inability to keep a commitment after it has been made.

It is absolutely essential for the leader of the group to protect the participants from disclosing information about themselves that might be used against them at some later date. For example, persons who have backgrounds or current experiences in incest, homosexuality, or criminal acts are often rejected or

exploited by others. Problems related to these experiences are best dealt with in private counseling.
A responsible leader of a TA church group remains
alert to this possibility and switches subjects if it
seems appropriate to protect someone from revealing
too much about himself.

The pastoral counselor also needs to know his own
limitations and how his own personality and background might affect a counseling group. He needs to
be aware of the limitations of his training. He knows
that an advanced degree in psychology or in a related field, and a legal license to practice counseling
are often important prerequisites.

The responsible pastor recognizes when individuals
are seriously depressed, disoriented, or out of touch
with reality in some way, and refers them to other
professionals who have more time, more training, or
both. He does not feel inadequate when he makes a
referral because he knows who he is and why he is
where he is. He seeks out professional consultation
and supervision so that when counseling others he
is as effective as possible.

A TA GOAL

One of the strengths of transactional analysis is
its rational approach to understanding individual
personality and interpersonal relationships. TA is a
tool a person can learn to use with increasing skill.
For men or women who like to use their hands, TA is
like a new kind of tool that they can use to construct
a new way of thinking. To men or women who like
to cook, TA is like a new kind of recipe book that can
be used to get more satisfaction out of living.

TA is also a tool a church can use. It helps free
people from some of their hangups so they can love
more adequately. In the beginning was God; in the
beginning was *Love*. To understand ourselves and
others is to experience the beginning *now*, in the
present moment, *here*, right here, wherever a few of
us are gathered together.

Though we are
born for love, others
may have neglected to
give it to us—and we
may have neglected to
give love to others.

EXERCISES IN RELEVANCY
(For Individual Use)

1. *Measuring Your Love Quotient*

Refer back to Chapter 1. Carefully reread the section on contracts, especially on the dimensions of love. In Fig. 2.1 place a dot opposite the number that reflects your loving quotient in each of the five dimensions.

Draw a line connecting the dots, then ask yourself:

- Am I satisfied with my loving ability? Why?
- Am I dissatisfied with my loving ability? Why?
- What am I willing to do to increase my love quotient?
- When am I going to start doing it?
- How will I follow through?

Try the experience several times with different people in mind, then ask:

- What differences do I notice?
- In what areas do I need to focus additional love energy?
- What steps do I need to take to achieve my goals?

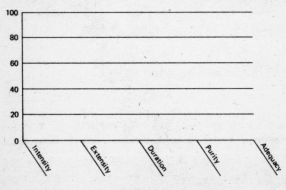

Figure 2.1

2. *Potluck Memories*

Plan to take about 10 minutes for this.

- Sit down in a comfortable chair in a quiet place. Slowly, slowly take a few deep breaths. Close your eyes and go back in memory to the last potluck or similar event you attended at a church. See yourself walking into the room, greeting people, finding a place to sit, and so forth. In your memory look around the room, see how it is arranged, who is there, and what they are doing.

- Try to be particularly aware of any unhappiness or tensions you observe or intuit. Stay with these memories until some understanding of the causes begins to emerge from within you.

- Next focus your awareness on the moments of joy or of understanding. Stay with these memories until some understanding of the causes begins to emerge from within you.

- Ask yourself: "Did everyone enjoy the potluck?" If not, what might have been planned differently so that they would have had a good time and felt accepted?

- Now ask what *you* could have done differently. Try to avoid being either defensive or judgmental.

3. *Your Birth and Your Name*

A birthday is a recognition of the day you were born. In many families there are brief stories about significant events surrounding a birth. Parents may make comments such as, "That was the day of a huge storm, so we named you Gale," or "We almost didn't make it to the hospital in time," or "When you were born you were exactly what I wanted," or "It was so painful I'll never forget." In addition to stories surrounding your birth there may have been parental expectations implied in your name. For example, persons with biblical names are often expected to model themselves after the Bible character who bore that name.

Your birth, the names you were given, subsequent nicknames of affection, or derogatory terms you were called have all been factors in shaping your personality. Ask yourself:

- Was anything said about my birth?
- Did I feel wanted as a child?
- Did my name have a special meaning?
- Did I like my name or not?
- Was I called something else? If so, did I like it?
- What effect did my birth and names have on me?

4. *Your Childhood Birthdays*

Some people have favorite ways to celebrate birthdays; some prefer to ignore them. This exercise will help you get in touch with childhood experiences which may have affected your current attitudes and actions.

- Once more get comfortable. Become aware of how your body feels, how your senses tune in or tune out the surrounding environment. Close your eyes for a minute or two.
- Imagine you have videotape equipment and tapes that have recorded all the events of your life. Imagine one of the tapes is labeled "Birthdays." Put the tape on the machine and project your scenes of childhood birthdays onto an imaginary screen. If your tape shows other people's birthdays watch those, too. Look at what the people are saying and doing.

Now ask yourself:

- What was the emotional climate? Artificial gaiety? Sadness? Unpleasantness? Genuine joy? Or what?
- What contributed to the happiness or unhappiness?
- How does the childhood event affect your life today?

5. *Recognitions and Celebrations*

Think of several people or organizations you know.

- Did you ever hope to receive a card, a phone call, or a gift from one of them and wait in vain? What was the occasion? How did you feel? Disappointed? Angry? Depressed? Or what? What did you do with your feelings? Repress them? Scold yourself for having them? Save resentments toward the person? Tell the person how you felt? Or what?

- Have you ever thought of sending a card, making a phone call, or taking a gift to someone and yet not doing it?
- Did your not doing it affect the relationship in any way?
- What excuse did you make to the person or to yourself?
- How do you imagine the other person felt if he or she was hoping to hear from you?
- Do you need to recognize special events and celebrate now?

EXERCISES IN RELEVANCY
(For Group Use)

6. *Memory Tapes*

Leaders of study groups may wish to review the notes addressed to them at the beginning of the book, then lead the groups on a memory trip. Use the following instructions, and pause after each direction.

- You will need to relax, get in a comfortable position, and close your eyes. Take time to let your memory flow back to a potluck or similar social event in the church.
- See the situation again as though it was being shown on videotape. Look at yourself walking in, greeting or avoiding people, making conversation, finding a place to sit, and so forth.
- Now, in your memory, notice the other people. What are they wearing? What are they doing? Can you hear what they're saying?
- Now try to re-experience the "emotional climate." Was it warm? Cold? Indifferent? Boring? Exciting? Did everyone seem to be enjoying it? If so, why? If not, why not?

After the memory exercise is concluded, open discussion can follow. If feelings of antagonism and resentment arise, work them through instead of suppressing them. Everyone's point of view has some value. Antagonism is usually related to a conflict in values and the subsequent struggle for control—to prove one's values are right and the other person's values are wrong.

7. *The Generation Gap*

In many churches young people are thought of as different, as less than full members because of age, hair length, clothes, behavior, and so forth.

- Consider your own church. How many youths hold decision-making positions on the official committees, including finance. How were they chosen? Are their opinions sought out on issues not directly related to youth? If no young people are on the important committees, why not?
- Now consider the opposite end of the generation gap—those who are at or past retirement age. Ask the same questions as above.
- How about those members in their 30's, 40's and 50's? Do they associate primarily with those in the same age bracket? If so, there's a gap. Does anything need to be done about it?
- Have an impromptu panel of people of different ages speaking on the generation gap as they experience it.

8. *Birthday Celebrations*

The biblical stories of the shepherds and wise men going to celebrate the birth of Jesus are among the best loved in Christian tradition. What specifically is done in your church at Christmas?

- Is it a genuine celebration? A nostalgic manipulation? What?
- Is it considered a chore or a joy to prepare for?
- Do people take a vacation from church afterward? If so why?
- Is it important to those who participate? What data do you have to support your opinion?

- Think of several people not in the church. Why might they be attracted to or why might they be turned off by Christmas in your church?
- Is any recognition given to people on their birthdays, such as was done at First Church?
- If so, is any effort made to discover what the person would like (e.g., pie instead of cake)? Does the recognition make the person feel happy?
- If no recognition is given to people's birthdays, why not? Is the reason legitimate? A justification? Or what?
- Is more data needed to decide the pros and cons?

9. Role Playing and the Non-Church Attender

Role playing is one of the most effective ways to discover what other people are thinking and feeling. It does not require acting ability or written lines, just a little intuition and willingness to try.

- Ask the study group to subdivide into smaller groups of from two to five persons.
- Ask each group to spend 10 to 15 minutes deciding on a situation in which non-church attenders would be discussing why they don't go. Let the focus be on social events, such as a potluck, and on major celebrations such as Easter and Christmas. One situation might be two men at work, another could be a family, a third might be among friends over coffee. Each group chooses its own roles and situation and then role plays them for the larger group.
- After the performance discuss the arguments that were presented. Were some of them valid? If so what can be done?

10. Designing a Joy Celebration

In every group there are creative people with good ideas about how to bring love, joy, and laughter into a situation. In most groups there are also some who, because of pain, despair, worry, or loneliness, have forgotten the feeling of joy. Yet each person, if en-

Celebrations in the church can be offered and received
with joy and meaning—or they can be a perpetuation
of customs that are not understood. When church
kindergartners sweetly carol "While shepherds wash their
socks at night," they have little comprehension of
shepherds and flocks, and grown-ups may laugh
indulgently at such naiveness. But while a carol, like
many hymns, may do little for the theological education
of the children, it may do much for their feeling
of being accepted as part of the church.

couraged, will have some ideas of joy and its meaning in a church.

- Go into small groups of from three to five persons.
- Let each group design a joy celebration.
- One group may think of the various ways of touching (for example, take a partner, close your eyes, and get to know your partner just by touching hands). Many resource materials are available on the use of touch. A small group might try them out before recommending them to others. Because many people have been mistreated physically in their childhood, and many others have been trained with statements such as "don't touch," the reluctance of these persons to touch or be touched must be seriously considered.
- Another group may think of how music could be used to bring joy to the heart. Different types of music will lead different people to feelings of joy.
- An evening of movies where classic cartoons are shown may gladden the hearts of many.
- A sunrise hike in silence may free some to drink in the joy of creation.
- Encourage each group to expand their traditional ways of doing things by letting their imaginations flow freely. Get all ideas without censoring any.
- Later evaluate the ideas. Don't try for the "perfect" one.
- Have many celebrations.

YOU CAN UNDERSTAND PERSONALITY

BEHIND THE SCENES

Tom Hardy, age 38, had been pastor of First Church for six years. He had taken the position after having served as associate pastor at the large Memorial Church a good day's drive away. Some of his church members said he was too liberal, others claimed he was too conservative. His budget committee called him very practical. Those who came for counseling found him helpful. His secretary thought he was a good boss. The high school group liked him because he didn't put down their interests and didn't preach to them when they asked questions. After a Sunday morning worship, members of the congregation often could—and did—say, "That was a good sermon, it really made me think." Some of the men praised him as a good preacher, a few claimed he was a better golfer. Occasionally some of the women of the church compared their husbands to him, with their husbands coming out second best. Without question, Tom Hardy was remarkably well liked in the local church.

Furthermore he was appreciated by his denominational officers and had served them effectively on several committees over the past few years. Tom was also sought out for membership in interfaith groups. He had developed the skill of really perceiving people's feelings, as well as listening to their words, and responding to both with sensitivity.

Each year Tom Hardy's church gave him two weeks

of paid study leave in addition to his vacation. He put it to good use. One year he would try to get caught up on the new trends in theological thinking and biblical study. On alternate years he would study educational methods, psychological theory and application, and sociological change. During his most recent study leave he had studied transactional analysis. In the process of learning it Tom Hardy had become aware of some of his own emotional needs that he tended to ignore. He realized for the first time that occasionally "just one more meeting" would be the one too many, or that one more phone call could be his breaking point. So he developed a capacity to say "No" occasionally. As Joe, the youth minister, put it, "Tom Hardy really keeps his cool."

Today, however, things had not gone well at the Hardy home. Three-year-old Susie had come down with a case of the sniffles and couldn't go to the nursery school. Betty, his energetic wife, had gone to her part-time job assisting in the mental health clinic. She was expected to be there two days a week until noon.

One time Betty had lamented, "I've just got to do this work if only to get away from the phone. It's hard not to answer when it rings, yet when I do, everyone expects me to say 'Yes' just because I'm a minister's wife."

Now Pastor Hardy didn't know whether Betty worked to avoid answering the phone and hearing the requests for help or not. He suspected that she enjoyed being independent more than she wanted to admit. He also knew it was imperative for her to be at the clinic on her scheduled day. Yet, today the usual babysitter had been unable to come and Tom was left with the problem of getting a substitute sitter.

On the way to the church he found himself feeling resentful, driving too fast and a little too carelessly. His face flushed when a member of the church board looked at him with raised eyebrows as Tom raced through a yellow light.

After arriving at his office, feeling embarrassed and anything but cool, Tom flung himself into the large overstuffed chair behind his desk and tried to recall his feelings during last night's potluck. He remembered these feelings had been quite ambivalent.

PERSONALITY THEORY

Having ambivalent feelings is not unusual. Dr. Eric Berne maintains that every person has three separate sources of feelings and behavior within him. These are called the Parent, Adult, and Child ego states (Fig. 3.1). They are not abstract concepts, he says, but realities that can be observed. "Parent, Adult, and Child represent real people who now exist or who once existed, who have legal names and civic identities."[1]

In TA, the method for analyzing the Parent, Adult, and Child ego states which comprise the structure of individual personality is called Structural Analysis. This is the technique for pinpointing and sorting a person's thoughts, feelings, and behavior. It teaches a person to understand himself and *change what he wants to change*.

When they are capitalized in this book, the words

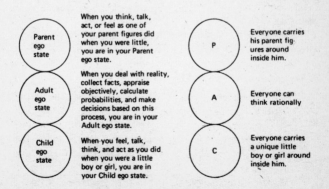

Parent ego state	When you think, talk, act, or feel as one of your parent figures did when you were little, you are in your Parent ego state.	**P** — Everyone carries his parent figures around inside him.
Adult ego state	When you deal with reality, collect facts, appraise objectively, calculate probabilities, and make decisions based on this process, you are in your Adult ego state.	**A** — Everyone can think rationally
Child ego state	When you feel, talk, think, and act as you did when you were a little boy or girl, you are in your Child ego state.	**C** — Everyone carries a unique little boy or girl around inside him.

Fig. 3.1 A simplified personality structure diagram

Parent, Adult, and Child will refer to ego states. When they are not capitalized, they will refer to actual parents, adults, and children.

The *Parent ego state* contains the attitudes and behavior copied from external sources, primarily from parents. Outwardly the Parent is expressed toward others in the kinds of critical and nurturing behavior that the person perceived his own parents using when he was young. Inwardly it is expressed much like recorded or taped messages which are heard by the inner Child and continue to influence it.

The *Child ego state* contains all the natural needs, impulses, and unique capacities with which a person is born. It also contains the effects of conditioning, training, and traumas a person experiences in early childhood; how he learns to respond to his training, and the positions taken about himself and others. The Child ego state is felt and is expressed in later life as "old" (archaic) behavior from childhood.

The *Adult ego state* refers to the ability to think rationally. When using the Adult, a person makes decisions and computes probabilities on the basis of facts, not on the basis of feelings or unverified opinions. The Adult ego state does not always make accurate decisions. There may not be enough facts available for it to do so. However, when using his Adult ego state a person does work objectively with the facts that he has. Using the Adult is his data processing and probability estimating ability. Everyone has it, even people who choose not to use it.[2]

TOM'S SELF-ANALYSIS

Pastor Hardy was able to analyze his feelings about the potluck because he could activate his Adult ego state, recognize his feelings, and estimate their validity. As though working with the pieces of a jigsaw puzzle, he could fit the data together and discover the picture.

First, he had shown paternalistic approval toward the group as a whole. This was very similar to behavior often expressed by his father, who had also been a pastor. According to TA theory, Tom's pater-

*nalistic response was from his Parent ego state be-
cause it was behavior copied from his father.*

Second, he had noted the contrast between the old
hymns—many of which had lost their significance
because of the outmoded language—and the new
style folk music which antagonized those who preferred tradition. He wondered if the conflict on
music indicated that the church was in a rut or out
of date, if he needed to do something to change it,
and if so what. According to TA theory, Tom's ana-
lytical thinking about music was a function of his
Adult ego state trying to estimate the situation rationally, much as a computer could do if given
accurate and sufficient data.

Tom's third feeling was one of resentment. This
contradicted both of his other responses. Wondering
what the congregation would say if he, their pastor,
should play the guitar, he felt that they would disapprove (though he had no data for this assumption)
and resented it. This was a familiar response for
Tom. In his childhood he had often incurred dis-
approval from his father's congregation when he tried
anything new. From these childhood experiences he
assumed his own congregation would treat him in a
similar way. Tom's third response was from his Child
ego state because his current feeling of resentment
was based on an archaic experience. He had not
checked it out to see whether he was right or wrong.

After sorting himself out Tom took a deep breath
and with fresh awareness said to himself, "That's why
I feel confused! My Parent, Adult, and Child each
had different responses. At least I solved that mys-
tery." He began to chuckle, "Here I am again, one
of the Hardy Boys I used to read about as a kid. I'm
still trying to solve mysteries. It must be part of my
script."

DEVELOPMENT OF EGO STATES

Ego states do not develop in sequence. Rather, the
development of one somewhat overlaps the development of another.

When first born, an infant's awareness centers around his own needs and comforts. He seeks to avoid painful experiences. He responds at the feeling level with whatever he has and is. His unique Child ego state emerges.

The Parent ego state begins to develop early in life as the young child observes its parents. A little girl who mothers her dolls is developing a nurturing parental function. The little boy who scolds his sister for spilling milk is setting the kind of limits for her that his parents have already set for him. Each is performing parenting functions that he has observed in his own parents.

The Adult ego state begins to develop in a child as he starts to gather information from his own world through his experiences and tries to figure out how to use this information. This skill starts to develop early in life, so everyone has an Adult ego state, including a young child. Every person, unless severely brain-damaged, is capable of using his adult data-processing ability if this ability can be activated.

The question of mature versus immature thinking and behavior is irrelevant. In transactional analysis the word "immature" is not used. What some people label immature is actually behavior which emerges directly from the Child ego state at inappropriate times.

All people have the potential to feel, smell, touch, speak, listen, observe, and act from each ego state. Each ego state has its own programming and its own value. Therefore, a person's three ego states may respond to a specific stimulus in quite different ways. Sometimes the ego states are in accord. Sometimes they are in conflict.

TA IN A COUNSELING SITUATION

When Mrs. Pillar stormed into the pastor's study, she was obviously angry. Pastor Hardy tried to listen while she exploded. Yet in the face of her anger, even though he tried to hear her out, he found himself getting hostile. Tom felt as if he were being per-

sonally criticized, though she said very little about him.

Because of his recent training in transactional analysis, Tom tried to examine his silent anger by asking himself the question "Why am I so upset because she doesn't like the kid's music?" Once more he began to get in touch with some of the feelings in his own ego states. He realized that the Child in him felt threatened when she "came on strong." This was one way his mother had often treated his father. At the same time he became aware that he was thinking about his problems, which he thought he had worked through, rather than about hers. So he refocused his attention from his Adult ego state and listened without interruption while she continued her mild tirade.

After a few minutes Tom picked up a small blackboard which he kept leaning against his desk, and, holding it in his hands so that Mrs. Pillar could also see, drew three circles, indicating the three ego states. From this blackboard diagram he explained the ego state structure. In a nonjudgmental way he helped her to understand which of her attitudes and statements came from her Parent ego state and which came from her Child. This was objective information that Jean Pillar could think about, and Pastor Hardy's lack of condemnation helped her do this without becoming defensive.

Jean learned quickly. She immediately became involved in the puzzle of finding out why she had different responses. After awhile a sudden look of comprehension came over her face. Almost grabbing the blackboard out of Tom's hands, she picked up the chalk and pointed toward the circle representing the Parent ego state. "This is what was going on inside of me! If my mother had been there, she would have said, 'Those kids should be singing hymns.' So part of my feeling about the folk music must have been similar to the way my mother felt. Yes, if my mother had been there last night, she would have been very critical about folk-singing in the church."

The Parent ego state begins to develop very early in life, when children start to copy their parents' behavior. They parent their dolls as they were parented, or parent other people in similar ways.

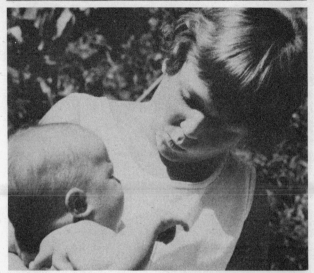

Above: Children, as well as grown-ups, have Adult ego states. This means that they can think logically, usually by the time they are seven years old. They may not have enough data to make accurate decisions—but this is often true of grown-ups, too. It's the process of thinking logically that indicates that the Adult ego state is functioning.

Right: The child ego state is a reflection of the free, uncensored parts of the personality and the trained, adapted parts. Some children are trained to be overly compliant, while underneath the compliance may be strong feelings of rebelliousness.

"You know, Pastor," and a wistful note crept into her voice, *"I had to go to church every week, twice a week in fact, when I was a little girl. It wasn't fun. It was boring. I often wished I could have been out playing instead of singing those same old hymns. It must have also been the Child in me that felt jealous last night. When I was little no one ever complimented me no matter how hard I tried and I always felt like an outsider.*

"Yet I do know that styles of church music are changing and that they need to change if we are to attract young people to the church. In fact, I saw some of these folk singers on T.V. last week. They were interesting and the words of the song really made me think.

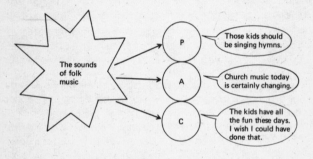

The sounds of folk music

P — Those kids should be singing hymns.

A — Church music today is certainly changing.

C — The kids have all the fun these days. I wish I could have done that.

Jean Pillar's responses to folk music

"You're right, Tom, there were different opinions, thoughts, and feelings going on inside of me almost at the same time.

"So that's what Transactional Analysis is all about," she said laughing. *"Well the church budget paid your registration fee for that TA seminar and workshop you went to last spring. Maybe you should teach a course in it here in the church. Plenty of people could use it."*

Pastor Hardy relaxed, *"Jean, you're really OK. I'm feeling better myself now that we've talked. In fact, I'll tell you something. Tom, our 13-year-old, has been* asking for a guitar and lessons. We just haven't been able to think clearly about it. . . ." Mrs. Pillar interrupted, "Now, just because I'm beginning to understand what makes me tick, don't think for one minute that I approve of guitars in the church. No sir, not for one minute!"

Just then the phone rang and Mrs. Pillar left abruptly with a slight smile. As Pastor Hardy answered the phone, a voice on the other end started speaking rapidly and a look of disbelief passed over Tom's face. "I'll be there as soon as I can," he said, "I'll leave the office right now." He hung up the phone. His head dropped till it rested on his arms. "Oh, my God," he moaned. Minutes later he stood up, took a deep breath and started for the office of his secretary, who had arrived while he and Mrs. Pillar were talking.

As Tom hurried down the hall, Austin Tenor, the choir director, approached him in agitation. "Tom, I'm so upset about what happened at last night's potluck supper! Last night I thought everything was OK, but today it looks much different to me. I've got to talk to you."

"I just can't talk right now, Austin. You know Sally Walker, the high school moderator, don't you? She was just killed in an auto accident. I have to stop by the office then hurry on out to the Walkers'. We'll just have to talk later."

"Good Lord, how awful," said Tenor. "Of course, Tom, you go ahead. I understand." He left the pastor and went into the chapel. As he slouched down onto the organ bench his thoughts were conflicting. The concern he felt about the previous evening and the things he had been going to say to Tom Hardy were all distorted by his agitation at the news of Sally Walker's death. True, he had not known her very well, but she was an active church member, after all, and by no means a stranger. And yet, he had wanted very much to talk to the pastor about something that was important to him, and he was quite disappointed that the opportunity had been postponed. The fact

*that he had been put off because of another person's
death did not ease the hurt of his rejection. To his
credit, Austin recognized the difference in importance
between what he had wanted to do and what had
prevented him from doing it, and he thought "What's
the matter with me, anyway? How come I feel hurt
so easily?"*

ENERGY SHIFTS IN EGO STATES

Each ego state is a separate and distinct entity.
In response to new stimuli, a person's psychic energy
can flow from one ego state to another through the
ego state boundaries, which are like semipermeable
membranes. This is what happened in the case of
Mrs. Pillar when she heard the folk music at the
supper. And in the case of Tom Hardy when she
expressed her anger to him. And to Austin Tenor
when he was put off by Tom's emergency call.

Different feelings may be evoked, often followed
by a change in behavior. Within a moment, a person's
posture, tone of voice, voice inflection, and facial
expressions can shift.

Each person has his own unique patterns of responding to new stimuli. The psychic energy of some
people, if they are confronted, observed, or opposed
by someone else, rushes to the Child ego state. In
others the same stimulus may activate the Parent in
them. Still others may respond from their Adult.
Regardless of which ego state a person's psychic
energy is in at a specific time, he usually feels this
is "really me, my thoughts, feelings, opinions," etc.
and is unaware of which part of his personality is
controlling him.

AUSTIN TENOR'S EGO STATES

*Many people, if they feel caught in childlike be-
havior, try to hide it to protect their public image.
For example, Mr. Tenor felt he didn't dare show his
feelings but had to swallow them when Tom Hardy
said he was too busy to talk to him. He had also tried*

to hide his feelings the night before but had been only partially successful. Joe, the youth worker, had caught on.

What had happened at the potluck was that Mr. Tenor had first responded good-naturedly to the young people with their guitars. Beneath his smiling approval were genuine feelings of good-will. He really did like young people. It was only after their successful performance as a folk group introduced by Joe that his feelings changed. This change was a definite shift of psychic energy in his ego states.

Earlier, Mr. Tenor had led the congregation seated at the dinner tables in a song fest beginning with "Row, row, row your boat" and on through a childhood favorite of his, "The Old Rugged Cross." Trained as a musician, he felt uncomfortable with this type of music, so it was not surprising that his leadership of the songs at the potluck supper lacked enthusiasm. Even when he had urged "Come on now, all together! Let's make this chorus a good one!" people had kept on talking.

Later, when the young people played their own folk selection, there was a lot of enthusiastic clapping from parents and other young people still seated at the tables. It was a threat to Tenor. "What's so great about guitars?" he verbalized internally. "How come nobody clapped for me!" With this, he had given his knee a hard whack, an old habit that emerged sometimes when he was feeling angry.

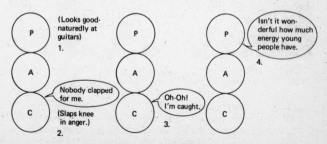

Austin Tenor's shift in ego states

Everyone has a Parent ego state containing attitudes
and actions copied from one's parent figures.
People tend to parent their children as they were
parented; they use nurturing and punitive behavior
as they experienced it. However, as some parental
behaviors and attitudes are prejudicial, ineffective,
or irrational, and others are protective, helpful,
and constructive, all of them need to be evaluated.

Everyone has an Adult ego state which has the capacity to think rationally and make logical decisions. Everyone also has the ability to use their Adult as the executive of their personality. As executive, the Adult can process data and use parts of the Parent and the Child as they are appropriate.

Everyone has a Child ego state which can add warmth and fun to the personality. Everyone has the birthright to live, laugh, and love. If, through physical deprivation or emotional mistreatment, this birthright is repressed, suppressed, or forgotten, it can still be recovered.

*Hearing the sound of hand on knee, Joe Miles, the
young minister, had looked up in surprise from his
place across the table and caught a glimpse of hurt
feelings and anger on Mr. Tenor's face. Seeing Joe's
look of surprise, Bill Tenor's face reddened. He was
embarrassed at being "caught" not living up to his
image of a church choir director.*

DIAGNOSIS OF EGO STATES

Ego states can be diagnosed in four different ways;
by a person's behavior (posture, voice, facial expressions, gestures, words, etc.), by his history (especially
what happened to him in his childhood), by observing
how others respond to him (enjoying, ridiculing,
correcting, exchanging information, etc.) and by the
subjective re-experience of feelings that were strongly
felt at some previous time in a similar circumstance.

Behavioral diagnosis includes awareness of each
ego state. Behavior that reflects the use of the Parent
ego state is sometimes expressed with authoritarian
words, voice, gestures, e.g.: scowling, shaking a finger
at someone, commanding "you must," "you should,"
"you have to," etc. Parent behavior is also expressed
in nurturing, tender ways, e.g.: patting someone on
the shoulder, smiling indulgently, giving unsolicited
but well meaning advice, using encouraging words,
etc.

Behavior reflecting use of the Adult ego state is
straightforward and focused on reality testing, e.g.:
working efficiently, asking direct questions, giving
straightforward answers, computing information.

Behavior reflecting use of the Child ego state is
like the behavior of a young child, e.g.: pouting,
having temper tantrums, giggling, teasing, expressing
oneself with "Gimme," "I don't care," "Wow."

Historical diagnosis is the identifying of a particular past event or person which contributed to an
individual's unique personality development or to his
patterns of interpersonal relations. For example, a
boy who is ignored by an overly busy father may
react, if his own children want his attention, pre-

cisely as his father did. A girl deserted temporarily by her parents or losing one through death may, when grown up, live in constant fear of her spouse leaving her.

Social diagnosis focuses not on what the person does, but on the response others have to him. For example, if a person is surrounded by others who continually ask him for advice or help, he is likely to be coming on from his Parent ego state to them more than he realizes. A person who feels competent himself, seeks others who are also competent, and exchanges information with them on the basis of mutual respect is likely to be in his Adult ego state most often. A person who continually responds to others as though they were the voice of authority or who resists taking responsibility for his own life is likely to be in the Child ego state most often.

Subjective or *phenomenological diagnosis* is validated by the re-experiencing of childhood feelings in a similar situation. For example, a person who in childhood was badly frightened by thieves robbing his house may, when fully grown, re-experience the terror and the need for protection if verbally attacked by a group of men. A person frightened as a child by a snake or dog may re-experience a similar feeling when meeting a snake or a dog. Conversely, pleasant experiences from the past may also be relived. Singing a beloved hymn may flood an older person with the same feelings of commitment to a cause that he experienced in his high school church group many years previously.

USE AND MISUSE OF EGO STATES

Each ego state is of value. Each can be used appropriately to enhance life, to add joy to it, to show concern for others. However each can also be misused. Misuse occurs if an ego state is overused or is unduly repressed. In such cases the ego boundaries are thick and rigid instead of being like permeable membranes through which the psychic energy can flow.[3] This is diagrammed as shown in Fig. 3.2:

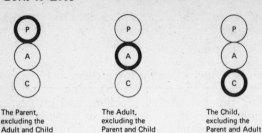

The Parent,
excluding the
Adult and Child

The Adult,
excluding the
Parent and Child

The Child,
excluding the
Parent and Adult

Fig. 3.2 Rigid ego boundaries

The Child ego state has great value when used appropriately to express curiosity, creativity, feelings of sexuality, affection, and self-protection.

It is misused if free and natural behavior is overly repressed. Repression may occur in response to brutal or very critical parenting. The Child is also misused if it is over-expressed. Over-expression of the Child occurs if overly-indulgent parents refuse to set limits, or continually praise clowning, precocious sexuality, or some other form of acting out behavior. If parents do not give approval for rational thinking, children may, like Peter Pan, choose the never-never land of youth and refuse to grow up.

Another form of misuse of the Child ego state is found in people who are overly polite, who are unduly obedient to authority and whose behavior lacks spontaneity. Although a child who is not adapted to politeness may be socially unacceptable when grown, some adaptations by parents are irrational.

The Adult ego state is best used when acting as the executive of a person's personality by objectively computing data and acting. It is misused if a person is exclusively rational, unable to play, or to nurture others at appropriate times. People are more than computers and need to be able to use both their Child and Parent ego states.

The Parent ego state is useful in rearing children and sometimes, in parenting other adults. It contains the critical and nurturing characteristics of one's parents and often much of this is good. Cultural, family, and church traditions are passed on generation after generation through the Parent ego state.

The Parent ego state is misused when a person frequently functions to keep others dependent, and when he criticizes or nurtures them at inappropriate times. Clergy and other leaders often are accused of having this personality problem, and an increasing number of people are resentful of those who assume the parental posture.

Any person with one of these rigid ego state boundary problems may be sincerely unaware of it except in moments when he wonders why he has difficulties in interpersonal relations. This unawareness is because psychic energy is not flowing back and forth in response to new stimuli. The feeling of "Self," of "This is really me," can be in any ego state at any moment.

When Mrs. Pillar was feeling highly critical she was experiencing the sense of Self in her Parent ego state. When planning and preparing the dinner she experienced her Self in her Adult ego state. When feeling neglected and angry her psychic energy was in her Child and this, at that moment, was her real self.

CONTAMINATED THINKING

Another different but very common problem of ego state boundaries is what Berne calls contamination. All people experience this problem occasionally, some more frequently than others. Contamination occurs when the rational data processing function by the Adult ego state is interfered with by wishful or fearful Child feelings and delusions and/or by Parent prejudices.[4] This is diagrammed in Fig. 3.3.

One way the Adult is contaminated by the Child is when people believe something magical will happen to solve their problems. They wait and wait for a Santa Claus to come and give them their heart's desires. Santa Claus is sometimes interpreted as a new job, new degree, new spouse, new friend, new house, new car, new clothes, etc. As the Adult knows,

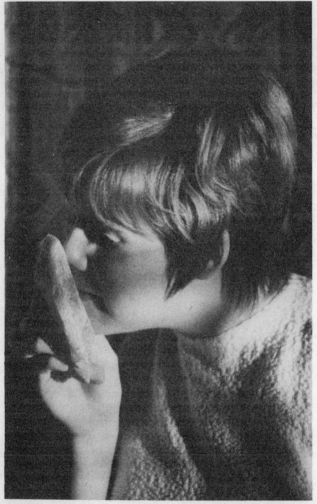

Sometimes all three ego states are active
at the same time; the Parent may plan good food
for the family, the Adult may check it for freshness,
and the Child may say "Mmmm."

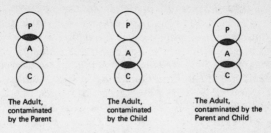

The Adult,
contaminated
by the Parent

The Adult,
contaminated
by the Child

The Adult,
contaminated by the
Parent and Child

Fig. 3.3 Contaminated Adult ego state

only in very rare instances do these things bring the ends wished for.

One way the Adult is contaminated by the Parent is when people believe they are usually right and that they are entitled to tell other people what to feel, what to think, and what to do.

Contamination is always related to specific situations or stimuli. For example, a man at work may function clearly and effectively from his Adult. Then when he goes home, if a touchy subject is broached by his wife or children, he may flip into contaminated thinking. Very few have this ego state boundary problem as a constant one. All people have it occasionally.

CONTAMINATED THINKING IN THE CHURCH

Lisa, the church soloist, had an Adult that was heavily contaminated by her inner Child in regard to her appearance. As a teenager she had been frequently told by her alcoholic father, "With your figure you could have anything." Consequently, Lisa lived her life under the delusion that her shapely figure would bring her happiness.

The opposite form of contamination—parental prejudices which interfere with the Adult—was a problem for Sam Morrison, the denominational executive. He was prejudiced about men and tended to categorize them as "hard workers" or "tramps" as his father often had. Sam was so deeply opposed to beards that despite all evidence to the contrary he once mumbled to Tom that all bearded men were "lazy bums who ought to be run out of the country."

However, neither Lisa nor Sam were always contaminated. In skill areas such as singing, housework, and sewing, Lisa functioned as a very adequate adult. Sam also had many areas in which he was uncontaminated. For example, he was strongly in favor of equal rights for women. On his staff women had the same salaries and benefits as men. When local churches asked for someone to fill the pulpit during their pastor's vacation, Sam often recommended a woman. In fact, he was a member of an ecumenical task force organized to study and make recommendations on the status of ordained women in the church.

Each member of the committee was assigned some in-depth interviews. One of Sam's interviews was with Suzanne Marshall, a pastor, who told him of several incidents in which she had experienced prejudice because of her sex.

Once when Suzanne was asked to be guest preacher at a local church, the deacon who phoned her remarked "What honorarium do you expect?" She replied, "Whatever you usually pay." "But," gulped the deacon, "you're a woman." "Yes, I know," she responded. "And you expect the same pay as a man?" he asked with a shocked, disapproving voice. "Why not?" she asked. "But you're a woman!" he repeated. "Yes, I know." And so the conversation continued with the line, "But you're a woman" being used to imply "you're not worth as much as a man."

Suzanne experienced a similar put-down when, in 1964 she decided to go to Selma, Alabama, where Martin Luther King, Jr., was leading a Civil Rights march. In her youth she had not directly experienced the problems and tragedies accompanying racial discrimination. Suzanne now wanted to see for herself. Yet when she called her denominational office to report her intent the same words, "But you're a woman," were used in an effort to discourage her going. One of Suzanne's theological convictions included Paul's admonition, "In Christ there is neither slave nor freeman, Jew nor Gentile, male nor female." She interpreted Paul as saying that if a person sees themself as "in Christ" the stereotypes of maleness and femaleness simply do not apply. She went and marched at Selma.

A third incident Suzanne had shared with Sam Morrison happened when she was asked by the bishop to be a guest at a large meeting of Episcopal clergy. After the bishop spoke, a rector asked, "How do you stand on the subject of the ordination of women?" The bishop replied, "After careful consideration of the Scripture I see no reason for not ordaining women, but the idea gives me a stomach ache." As he grasped his stomach to demonstrate his feeling, he looked out at the group, saw the one woman sitting in the back of the room and moaned, "Oh my God, there's Suzanne!"

Late that night Suzanne sat on the rocks by the ocean and struggled with the question of the validity of her own ordination. She remembered Paul: "In Christ there is neither male nor female. . . ." The bishop must have done the same, for the next morning he almost flew across the room to ask her forgiveness. Shortly after this event he put his words into action and ordained a woman deaconess.

Sam's ecumenical committee concluded that prejudicial thinking regarding women was passed on, generation after generation, from Parent ego state to Parent ego state, in both religious and secular cultures.[5] The committee discovered that the Greek myth of Pandora blames women for all evil, as does the biblical story of Eve; that the Greek philosopher Aristotle claimed women were an unsuccessful act of procreation; that the writer of the book of Job proclaimed a man could not be clean because he was born out of the uncleanliness of woman, that during the Reformation one of the subjects debated was "Are women human?"

While recognizing that prejudicial thinking about

*women was widely accepted partly because of its
long history, the committee knew that if love pervaded
the churches, discrimination in all forms—race,
ethnic background, religious affiliation, age, sex, etc.
—would disappear.*

A TA GOAL

All churches periodically evaluate their theology,
which is expressed both in word and in action. Historically, these same churches change on the basis of
what they discover. Transactional Analysis can be
used both for evaluation and to initiate desired
change.

Each person has unique Parent, Adult, and Child
ego states. The overuse or underuse of any ego state
is a common personality problem. Even more common is the contamination of Adult clear thinking by
Parental opinions and by Child feelings and adaptations. Understandably so, each person may feel, think,
and act differently at different times. The differences
between people can be interpreted as undesirable and
destructive or as part of the creation plan and therefore good. After all, in the beginning Love created
. . . and lo, it was good. The beginning is still here.
The beginning is now.

EXERCISE IN RELEVANCY

(For Individual Use)

1. Music in Childhood

The effect of music, lyrics, and rhythm on children
is well known. A lullaby may lull them to sleep, a
march may initiate their militant feelings, a "round"
may be sung in the hopes of developing *esprit de
corps*. For many people, their early musical experiences are important. Ask yourself the following
questions:

- What kind of music did I experience as a young
  child?

- Did I like it? Did other members of the family like it?
- Who controlled the use of music?
- Was anything said or inferred about some kinds being good and some being bad?
- What kind of music do I think each person in my family would have liked?
- If I sang or played an instrument did I enjoy it freely? Did I feel compelled to perform? Was it a solitary or group activity?

2. *Music Now*

To discover what effect, if any, your childhood musical experiences had on your later life, become aware of your current preferences. Ask:

- In church recently which hymns did I like?
- Which did I dislike?
- Are my likes and dislikes related to my childhood experiences?
- How would my parents respond to the hymns I liked or disliked?
- What other music have I been listening to?
- What ego states responded to the music?

3. *Psychic Energy and Ego States*

When a new stimulus (i.e., sound, sight, odor, etc.) enters a person's environment, the psychic energy, accompanied by the feeling of real self, may flow from one ego state into another. Close your eyes and try to recall the last twenty-four hours.

- Did any of my senses tune in to anything unusual?
- If so, was it pleasant (or not)?

Next try to recall a recent tense situation.

- Did I suddenly become angry? Depressed? Sad? Confused? Or what?
- If so, what was the stimulus that triggered the feeling?

- Where did my response come from? My Parent? My Adult? My Child?

Now think of a problem you recently solved.

- How did I do it? Was my answer based on my Child feelings? On my Parent traditions? On my Adult data processing?
- Which ego state was more closely involved in the problem?
- Which more clearly involved in the solution?
- Am I satisfied with my solution? If not, what can I do to redecide?

4. *Facing Conflict and Recognizing Anger*

Reread the section in which Mrs. Pillar is angry at Pastor Hardy. Make lists of people you could—or have—felt angry toward:

Angry at them in the past:	Currently angry or resentful toward:	Might be angry at them in the future:
_____	_____	_____
_____	_____	_____
_____	_____	_____
_____	_____	_____

- Now look at your lists. Try to see if there is any similarity between the types of people who "make" you angry, the types of situations which "make" you angry.

Blaming others for one's own feelings is common. But actually each person is responsible for his own feelings.

- To get in touch with this fact, say to yourself: "I am (or have been or will be) angry at you _____ , (name) and I take responsibility for it."

- Make this statement for each person on your list.
- Let the import of the words "and I take responsibility for it" sink in as you get in touch with your feelings.

5. Ego State Portrait

Using circles of different sizes draw your ego state portrait as you *perceive yourself* most of the time.[6] Your portrait might look something like Fig. 3.4.

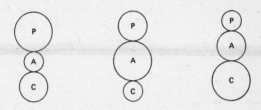

Figure 3.4

- Do you see yourself as having a favorite ego state?
- Does your portrait change when the situation changes? At work? At home? At school? At a party? Where else?
- Does it change with certain people? A boss? Subordinate? Spouse? Children? Friends? Who else?
- Now ask a child, spouse, friend, relative, and/or business associate to draw how he perceives you. Notice any differences?

After you have drawn your ego state portraits, both from your own perspective and that of others, ask yourself:

- Does this satisfy me? If not, what needs to be changed?

6. Designing a Private Sanctuary

One of the capacities that originates in the Child ego state is the ability to use imagination. If you sometimes feel exceedingly tired or in pain, or if you are with people who give off negative vibrations then you may need an imaginary sanctuary[7] where you will be protected and find rest. To prepare for this exercise, take time to get physically comfortable.

- Imagine being outdoors in your own special space. You may have anything in this space that you like, e.g., a stream, trees, flowers, etc.
- Next, imagine a wall around this space. The wall is the kind that makes you feel safe and cannot be penetrated. Let it be as high or low as you like but let it be open to the sky. It has one strong gate, you have the key.
- Now look around your space which you can change any time you like. If it needs anything to make it more like your private sanctuary, add it.
- Now imagine that you have a spiritual guide with you, and the function of this guide is to protect you, direct you, aid you, and comfort you.
- Ask your guide to protect you from negative vibrations, to clear your sanctuary of evil thoughts, to scrape them from the walls if they climb in, and send them out the gate.
- Imagine the gentle warmth of the sun is shining down upon you and a mild breeze touches your face.

The power of imagination is very strong. You will be able to return to this imaginary sanctuary at any time and replenish your energy and your ability to love.

EXERCISES IN RELEVANCY
(For Group Use)

7. *Recognizing Ego States*

- Make lists of words, phrases, postures, facial expressions, etc. that would be characteristic of each ego state.

Parent

_____   _____

_____   _____

_____   _____

_____   _____

_____   _____

Adult

_____   _____

_____   _____

_____   _____

_____   _____

Child

_____   _____

_____   _____

_____   _____

_____   _____

_____   _____

- In small groups discuss agreements and disagreements about the lists.

8. *Ego States and Music*

- Let each person in the group read over the first individual exercise, Music in Childhood, and jot down a few notes after each question.

- Then, as a group, discuss the various responses.
- Next, let those who are willing state how their ego states were activated during the discussion.

9. *Analyzing Hymns*

- Write down the name of one of your favorite hymns.
- In the blanks of Fig. 3.5 fill in (1) Parent (your Parent figures) opinions, attitudes on that hymn or type of hymn. (2) Your Child feelings and experiences about it. (3) Your Adult rational thinking about the music, words, and intent of the writer.

Figure 3.5

- Have group discussion. Use hymn books and carefully consider the words of those chosen by the group. Are they archaic? Sentimental? Nostalgic? A denial of reality? Designed to manipulate? Encouraging? What?
- What would be the various responses to these hymns of those who come to Sunday services only occasionally?
- Are you pleased with what you've discovered? If not, why not?

PICTURE A WELL-KNOWN HYMN

"Rock of Ages, cleft for me. . . "

What needs changing?

Who can do the changing?

When can they do it?

How can they do it?

Are they willing?

10. *Hymns and Photographs*

- Look closely at the accompanying photograph,
  which the photographer said reminded him of
  the old hymn "Rock of Ages Cleft for Me . . ."
- Collect art pictures, pictures from magazines, or
  your own photographs.
- Have an exhibit of the pictures. Name them
  according to the hymns they suggest to you.

11. *Ego State Responses*

In small groups have class members discuss possible ego state *responses* to each of the following
situations. Then have open class discussion so that
the diversity of answers can be enjoyed.

Situation 1: A committee chairman receives negative
newspaper publicity.

Parent

Adult

Child

Situation 2: The pastor comes down with flu when
faced with a difficult meeting.

Parent

Adult

Child

Situation 3: A member of the church has received an award for excellent performance.

Parent

Adult

Child

12. *Fantasy Trip to Childhood*

Let each person get into a comfortable position and close his or her eyes.

The group leader can read the following aloud slowly (take three to five minutes). Pause whenever there are three dots. Use a mild monotone voice so as not to interfere with the fantasy.

- "Let yourself go back into your childhood. See yourself as a young boy or girl. . . . Get reacquainted with where you lived between the ages of five and ten. . . . Look at the house or the apartment from the outside. . . . Walk in the front door. . . . Slowly explore the rooms. . . . See how the furniture is arranged. . . . See who is there and what they are doing. . . ."
- "Imagine that the parent figures there are willing to talk to you. . . . Ask them to define religion for you. . . . Ask them about the church. . . .

Ask them why they think the way they do . . .
now come back to the group."
- Next list on the board the various parent comments heard during the fantasy trip.
- Next discuss how each person's Adult and Child ego states would agree or disagree with what their Parent said in the fantasy.

13. Cultural Stereotypes

- Working in small groups of from four to six, discuss and list some commonly held stereotypes of men and women.
- Work quickly without evaluating and list the group's words in two columns.

Men are: Women are:

_____   _____

_____   _____

_____   _____

_____   _____

_____   _____

_____   _____

- Now compare your lists and note how many of the words or phrases used apply to persons of either sex.
- Now list five different jobs that are usually given to men or women, but seldom to both.

Think of what "reasons" are given for the choice and from what ego states the reason is given.
How many "reasons" are prejudicial contamination?

YOU CAN ANALYZE TRANSACTIONS

GRAND CENTRAL STATION

Myra was glad when she heard Pastor Hardy coming toward her office. It was a small all-purpose office and, as always happened on Fridays, it would get busier as the day wore on. In fact she sometimes thought of it as Grand Central Station. So many people coming and going—leaving messages with her, borrowing pencils, returning books, asking about announcements to be put in the church bulletin. By the end of a busy day she often found herself wishing that she could lock the door, pull down the shades, and sit there alone for just one hour. As she said to herself, "Sometimes it's hard to be 'Christian' and sometimes I don't even know what the word 'Christian' means." Myra's mother had told her the word meant Christ-like, which meant the willingness to suffer without complaint and always put other people's needs first. "But," thought Myra, "that kind of Christian is what I'm not—especially on Fridays."

It wasn't only the confusion of people coming and going that sometimes got to her, it was also the office itself. The mimeograph machine was old and often broke down. The file cabinet had a roller off one of the drawers and she had to be careful when pulling it out or it might drop to the floor, either spilling all the file folders or landing on her toe. And the church was having budget problems. Several of the pledging families had either dropped out of church or moved away, so Myra had been asked to conserve on heat and electricity in her office. Occasionally she felt cold

*and resented it. Then too, the inevitable reams of
paper for the weekly newsletter and the stack of
Sunday bulletins that always needed to be done on
Friday were always in the way somehow. Even her
desk was dwarfed by a big table which a deacon
used for folding Sunday bulletins and the treasurer
used regularly for counting out money and checking
the church accounts.*

*Mad at herself for not counting her blessings as
she had been taught to do as a child, Myra closed
her desk drawer with a bang just as Pastor Hardy
entered. Flustered, feeling "caught in the act," she
picked up the letters she had been typing. However,
one look at his face told her something was wrong.
Myra had worked with him long enough to read his
moods. "Is anything wrong, Tom?" she asked with a
note of concern in her voice.*

*"It's Sally," responded Tom slowly. "She was thrown
from a car in an auto accident. Now she's dead, Myra.
Bob was driving but wasn't hurt. It happened when
he swerved to avoid a bus, but his car skidded and
flipped over as he went down the bank by the over-
pass."*

*"Oh no!" gasped Myra as tears filled her eyes, "I
can't believe it! It can't be true. Not Sally! Not that
lovely girl!"*

*As they talked about the accident, Tom, holding
his head in his hands, lamented, "I feel so bad I can't
think." Finally he sighed, "What am I going to tell
their parents?"*

*"Oh Tom," Myra chided him gently, "you'll know
what to say. They'll need words of comfort and help
with the funeral arrangements and lots of help afterward. You know that."*

*"You're right, of course, Myra. I'm just badly
shaken. Sally's parents must feel like their world has
collapsed. So will the kids in the Youth Fellowship.
She was a great girl."*

*The two sat in silence; finally Myra reached over
and, like a nurturing parent, patted Tom on the arm.*

"Somehow we'll rally around the family and help while they go through this terrible time."

Tom Hardy stood up, straightened his shoulders, and went out to his car. Myra turned back to the typewriter and tried to put her mind on her work. Feeling guilty for her earlier resentment she became aware of her inner dialogue and heard again the words her father used to say. "Think of all you have to be grateful for."

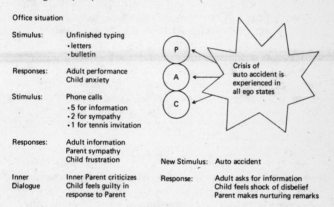

Office situation		
Stimulus:	Unfinished typing • letters • bulletin	
Responses:	Adult performance Child anxiety	
Stimulus:	Phone calls • 5 for information • 2 for sympathy • 1 for tennis invitation	
Responses:	Adult information Parent sympathy Child frustration	

Crisis of auto accident is experienced in all ego states

New Stimulus: Auto accident

Inner Dialogue	Inner Parent criticizes Child feels guilty in response to Parent

Response: Adult asks for information
Child feels shock of disbelief
Parent makes nurturing remarks

Multiple Input to Myra

TRANSACTIONS BETWEEN PEOPLE

When anything happens between two persons, such as the interchange of words and feelings between Myra and Tom Hardy, it involves a "transaction" between their ego states. Because each person has three ego states and each is different, there are many possible transactions. These transactions can be identified.

One part of the theory of Transactional Analysis is based on the fact that whenever one person speaks to another he is sending a transactional *stimulus* and is expecting some kind of *response*. The same is true whenever he shows specific behavior—he is sending a stimulus and expecting a response.

Behavior carries messages with it. For example, if one person gives another a frown, the message is "I disapprove of you." If a person weeps, the message is "Don't hurt me. Look how bad, sad, or hurt I'm feeling." If a person nods his head and smiles, the message is "I like or approve of you." If he laughs, he is showing amusement, pleasure, or good humor.

The messages that accompany behavior are more important than words, but as most people know it's not what you say, it's the way that you say it that really counts. Words and nonverbal messages may or may not be congruent. If they are congruent, realistic, and affectionate a person feels understood. He feels confirmed, alive, and may even feel free. If not, he feels ignored, put down, discounted, and may even feel half dead. In many churches there are those who do not act on the basis of their words of love. Instead they may try to manipulate others, try to control them as a parent might do or as a child might attempt to do.

Berne says there are three basic types of transactions: complementary, crossed, and ulterior. Every person engages in these three types from time to time. If words and behavior are congruent between two people, their transactions are complementary. If they are not congruent, the transactions are either crossed or ulterior.

COMPLEMENTARY-TRANSACTION THEORY

A transaction is described as complementary when a message, sent from an ego state in one person, gets an expected response from an ego state in another person. This is common in healthy relationships.

Complementary transactions can occur between any ego states. When they do, the lines of sending and receiving between persons are parallel and communication is open. There are nine basic types of complementary transactions. They occur between Adult and Adult, Child and Child, Parent and Parent, or Parent and Child. Complementary transactions can go on indefinitely unless someone gets tired or bored.

Complementary Transactions in the Church

At the potluck, Kathy, age 3, had run laughing to her cousin Raymond, age 13, thrown open her arms to him, and shouted "Here I am, you guy!" As she expected, Raymond had picked her up and swung her about. This was an affectionate complementary transaction from their Child ego states.

Occasionally complementary relationships are static instead of growth-enhancing. Such is the case if two individuals are locked into a stereotyped pattern of transacting. Lisa's marriage was like that. It was based on a strong Parent-to-Child relationship. The unspoken assumption between her and her husband was that he would take care of her like an indulgent parent and that she would act like a sexually precocious adolescent. Lisa's husband sensed the unhealthiness of this continuous Parent-Child relation, but Lisa refused to act differently. Their marriage was in danger.

The healthiest way of transacting with each other is to use all the complementary transactions but to

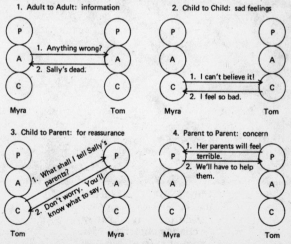

1. Adult to Adult: information
   1. Anything wrong?
   2. Sally's dead.
   Myra   Tom

2. Child to Child: sad feelings
   1. I can't believe it!
   2. I feel so bad.
   Myra   Tom

3. Child to Parent: for reassurance
   1. What shall I tell Sally's parents?
   2. Don't worry. You'll know what to say.
   Tom   Myra

4. Parent to Parent: concern
   1. Her parents will feel terrible.
   2. We'll have to help them.
   Myra   Tom

Summary of Tom and Myra's Complementary Transactions

Adult-to-Adult transactions
can occur between people
of different ages if they
exchange objective infor-
mation with each other.

Child-to-Child
transactions also occur
between people of different
ages who joke, laugh, fight,
or play together.

In healthy relationships, people transact openly and directly from any ego state and receive the reponses they expect. If one person uses a nurturing Parent transaction to the unhappy Child in someone else, then that unhappy Child ego state is likely to feel better.

People of any age can have complementary transactions between similar ego states, as when two people discuss parentally what should be done about "those kids," or "that church," or any subject of mutual interest.

*use whichever is most appropriate to the situation.
Tom's and Myra's working relationship was based
on this. It was always flexible, and that morning had
contained many complementary transactions[1] when
their words and actions were congruent.*

CROSSED-TRANSACTION THEORY

A transaction is defined as crossed if a message
sent from the ego state of one person gets an *unexpected* response from another. It is a transaction
in which something goes wrong. Such is the case if
one person directly asks, "What time is it?" and
receives a crossed response of a whining Child,
"Gee, I don't know. Why ask me?" or of a critical
Parent, "Why don't you wind your own watch!" or of
a nurturing Parent, "Just a minute and I'll go find
out for you."

Crossed transactions often lead to misunderstand-
ings, to hurt and angry feelings between people. They
occur in a family, on a job, at social gatherings, and
in a church. The person who is the recipient of a
crossed transaction often feels put down.

In response to this feeling he may withdraw while
fantasizing that he is misunderstood and that the
other person is incapable of understanding. Or he
may change the subject with "Let's talk about something else." Or he may instigate a fight with "Why
do you always do that when you know I don't like it?"

Although, according to Berne, there are many types
of crossed transactions that are possible, only about
four of them (see Fig. 4.1) occur frequently in daily
life.[1]

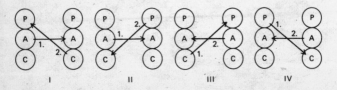

Fig. 4.1 Common Crossed Transactions

Crossed Transactions in the Church Office

Myra was just getting back to the office work that Pastor Hardy had interrupted with the bad news about Sally when Jean Pillar sailed in, holding high a vase in each hand. She intended to give Myra her firm opinions about the preschool nursery group.

Like Myra, Mrs. Pillar was efficient, but all too often she acted parental toward others and expected a childlike response of compliance from them. It was hard for her to understand people who "crossed" her and who rejected what she defined as "constructive criticism." When people responded to Mrs. Pillar with compliance, the transaction was complementary. When they didn't, it was crossed. A transaction is crossed if the stimulus from one person does not get the expected response from another, and Mrs. Pillar was often the instigator as well as the receiver of crossed transactions.

It was after her explosion in the pastor's study that Mrs. Pillar had gone downstairs to the kitchen to get vases for flower arrangements for the Sunday morning service. Most of her responsibilities were self-assigned: "After all, no one else is around to do these things." A few tasks were given her by committees who recognized her competence and justified their numerous requests with comments such as, "Jean Pillar's children are grown so she has more free time than younger mothers." Jean could always be counted on to do what she agreed to do, so people had a tendency to say, "Why not let Jean do it?"

She had heard teachers saying that the children became very restless before their parents picked them up after Sunday School. Some cried unhappily to go home; others became too boisterous with the toys; still others pounded on the piano, disturbing the class in the next room. Occasionally a child would try to run away. Consequently, the preschool class was sometimes obstreperous.

"Myra," said Mrs. Pillar forthrightly, "I think that

CROSSED TRANSACTIONS
LEAD TO
MISUNDERSTANDINGS

A transaction is crossed
when a given stimulus gets
an unexpected reaction.
Crossed transactions sometimes lead to confusion.

Crossed transactions
can also lead to anger if
people feel misunderstood
or "put down."

*those little children should have juice and crackers
Sunday morning. It will keep them quiet a little
longer."*

Myra smiled a greeting to Mrs. Pillar. She was
used to her abrupt ways and not upset by them. "I
don't see why not," she responded. "However, better
check with Mr. Pennyworth about the money for it."

Mrs. Pillar bristled. "I don't see any point of going
through all that. I thought I'd just buy the juice and
crackers and give the bill to Mr. Pennyworth. That's
less than two dollars a week."

"That's Jean," Myra thought. "Whenever she decides to do something, she just barges ahead. I
wonder what Mr. Pennyworth will say. He keeps
such tight control on the purse strings of the church
school treasury."

Just at that moment, before Myra had a chance
to speak, Mr. Pennyworth appeared in the doorway.
He was preparing a report on the budget committee
for that evening and was coming in to check over the
accounts to see whether or not the pledges were up
to date.

With his ear always tuned to money, he caught
Mrs. Pillar's ". . . less than two dollars a week," and
asked, "What's less than two dollars a week? That
adds up to over a hundred dollars a year, you know."

"Here we go again," thought Myra. "Here comes
another one of those clashes!"

"Well, it's like this," Jean Pillar said in her typically
blunt manner. "I've talked to several people and
we all think that the preschool class should have
juice and crackers on Sunday morning. Now, I'll give
you the bills every few weeks. It shouldn't be more
than two dollars a week. I can't see any reason for
arguing over that."

As the last few words were being spoken Mr.
Pennyworth's face reddened. Almost before she finished, he broke in vigorously, "Who do you think is
the treasurer around here? I can't authorize your bills.
As I've told you a dozen times, put your requests
through regular channels!"

At this point Myra slipped out of the office, murmuring aloud, although neither seemed to be listening to her, "I'm going to the post office to pick up some stamps." To herself she added, "I just can't take any more today."

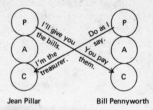

Jean Pillar   Bill Pennyworth

Summary of a Crossed Transaction

Myra and Pastor Hardy had talked about TA enough for Myra to have grasped the basics. Now she realized that Mrs. Pillar's statement came from her Parent ego state and was directed to Mr. Pennyworth as though he were a child who was always expected to agree. Instead, Mr. Pennyworth had crossed her up by responding from his Parent ego state, speaking to Jean as though she were the child.

"Well," mumbled Myra to herself, "at least I understand that transaction."

ULTERIOR-TRANSACTION THEORY

Ulterior transactions always have a hidden agenda. Sometimes they are dishonest. Under the guise of ordinary words, an indirect message goes from one person to another. When a transaction has an ulterior dimension it is communicated by posture, facial expression, tone of voice, inflection, gesture, etc.

There are two types of ulterior transactions, *angular* and *duplex.* An angular ulterior transaction involves one ego state in one person and two ego states in another. A duplex ulterior transaction involves two ego states in each person. In Fig. 4.2 these are diagrammed with the dashed line as the ulterior or covert message and the solid line as the verbal or

Ulterior transactions
are communicated by tone
of voice, gestures, posture,
and facial expressions.

In a moment an open fun-
loving child can become
a defiant child, and,
without words, send out a
"Try and make me" message.

overt message. The *ulterior stimulus* can be sent by facial expression, tone of voice, gestures, body posture, etc. from any ego state to any ego state.

When Tom talked and listened nonjudgmentally to Jean Pillar he offered information from his Adult to her Adult and nonverbal acceptance to her Child. When Lisa flirted with the men in the church she gave a sexually provocative Child-to-Child message while at the same time she was offering verbal Adult information.

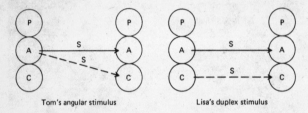

Tom's angular stimulus   Lisa's duplex stimulus

Fig. 4.2 Ulterior Stimulus Patterns

Myra's Analysis of Ulterior Transactions

On her way to the post office Myra was thinking about some of the transactions that had gone on that morning in her office. Mr. Pennyworth and Jean Pillar had met head-on in a crossed transaction over juice and crackers for the preschool class, but the misunderstanding between Mr. Pennyworth and Joe Miles the week before had an additional overtone to it.

"Poor Mr. Pennyworth," she was thinking. "He's retired, living on a limited income, feeling the pressure from rising food costs and taxes. Only last week he said that even his auto insurance had gone up. Maybe his personal worries about money carry over into his feelings about the church budget. He's a good man, even if he is sometimes too cross with people about church spending, and he means well and seems to want to protect the church school funds.

"And Joe. He's such a nice guy. He's always trying to help. For someone who's still studying in seminary, he puts in a lot more time than he gets paid for and

has a lot of good feelings for people. I'm glad when he drops in to talk to me." She recalled that last week he had said that he was living up to his image of "good ole Joe" by putting out a fire that had been started in the shed on the back of the church lot. The shed was used to store hoses and garden tools and sometimes Ed, the janitor, forgot to lock it. Ed was often a little forgetful and Joe said he was worried about the fire because of all the high grass around the shed.

Joe had phoned Mr. Pennyworth from Myra's office to report the fire and Mr. Pennyworth had gotten really angry, shouting so loud that Myra could hear him. "Hells bells, Joe! that shed's no good. Why didn't you let the damn thing burn? We've got insurance. Nothing else would really have been hurt. We could have got some money for a new shed out of that!"

Joe hadn't been able to believe his ears. Mr. Pennyworth actually wanted the shed to burn down. As Joe told Myra later, "All I could think of to say was, 'Gosh! Maybe you're right.' I felt really stupid."

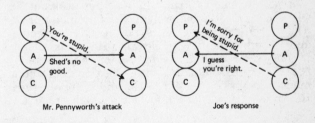

Mr. Pennyworth's attack   Joe's response

Summary of an Ulterior Transaction at First Church
(The broken lines indicate the ulterior message.)

In this transaction it was Mr. Pennyworth's Adult who had told Joe the shed was no good while his Parent called Joe's Child "stupid" by giving an ulterior message with his tone of voice. Joe's Adult had agreed about the shed while his embarrassed Child apologized.

OK AND NOT-OK THEORY

On the basis of early life transactions all children take psychological positions about themselves which are usually maintained at a feeling level throughout their lives unless they decide to change. The positions are either that they are OK as a person or that they are not-OK. They also take positions that other people are OK or not-OK.

These OK and not-OK positions are at opposite poles:

Rejection of self (I'm not-OK)	Acceptance of self (I'm OK)
Rejection of others (They're not-OK)	Acceptance of others (They're OK)

These polarities result in four basic positions: [3]
1. I'm (we're) OK, you're (they're) OK.
2. I'm (we're) OK, you're (they're) not-OK.
3. I'm (we're) not-OK, you're (they're) OK.
4. I'm (we're) not-OK, you're (they're) not-OK.

A person who is firmly in the first position, I'm OK, you're OK (the mentally healthy position), is one who is self-expressive, does not require perfection, and is both tolerant and flexible. He tends to have friends who feel similarly and seldom has an enemy. Because of his "get-along-with" position[4] he autonomously sets realistic life goals and achieves them. He knows he was born for love and born to love others.

A person who frequently expresses himself from the second position, I'm OK, you're not-OK (the arrogant or paranoid position), is critical, blames others if things go wrong, is a chronic advice giver, and may seek others to persecute physically or non-physically. Because of his "get-rid-of" position, he often drives friends, spouse, and children away. He erroneously believes that he is lovable and others are not.

A person in the third position, I'm not-OK, you're OK (the depressive position), frequently withdraws, helpless and depressed, refuses to take adequate responsibility for his own feelings and behavior, and expects others to rescue him. Because of his "get-away-from" position, he deserts, withdraws, or runs away from others emotionally and/or physically. He thinks he is unlovable and that only other people are worthy of love.

A person in the fourth position, I'm not-OK, you're not-OK (the schizophrenic or schizoid position), feels and acts as though nothing is worth while. Because of his "get nowhere" position he feels as if he never does anything right and that life isn't worth living. He is convinced that neither he nor anyone else is lovable.

The OK and not-OK positions can also apply to church groups. Churches who take the first double OK position (We're OK, You're OK) appreciate and respect the persons who comprise their own group as well as those who do not belong to their inner circle.

Other churches, however—both "liberal" and "conservative"—have, within church history, taken the second position. They have considered themselves, their rituals, their dogmas, their disciplines, their ordinations, their missionary concerns, even their buildings, to be OK and those of others to be not-OK.

At the same time, other church groups have sometimes taken the third position—we're not-OK, you're OK. Some of these churches who feel not-OK have tried to copy those they admire (e.g., liturgy and vestments). Or they have merged with other churches for survival or for power. Or they have withdrawn into themselves, using guilt-producing patterns of words and behavior within the congregation.

If a church takes a position of we're not-OK and neither is anyone else, it usually disintegrates in dismay.

OKness in the Church

All the people active in First Church—Joe, Myra, Mrs. Pillar, Mr. Pennyworth, Pastor Hardy and others —had their own personality idiosyncrasies. Each felt and expressed their joys, sorrows, angers, and despairs in different ways. Even their resentments and appreciations of the church, as well as of each other, were in some way affected by experiences, traumas, and transactions of their early childhood—especially those which occurred with their parent figures.

One of the reasons little Kathy and her cousin Raymond enjoyed seeing each other at the potluck and why Pastor Hardy and Myra could work together was that, although they disagreed at points, they had an "I'm OK, You're OK" position about themselves and each other. They had taken this position as a result of happy childhood.

In contrast, Mrs. Pillar tended to come on as a parent. Early in life she had had to assume great responsibility for her younger brothers and sisters when her mother died. She was so used to this role that she treated other grown-ups as though they were children. She gave the impression that she thought she had all the answers and was therefore OK and that they did not have the answers and therefore were not-OK.

Sometimes from her position of I'm OK, you're not-OK, Mrs. Pillar acted nurturing and helpful; sometimes she acted overly critical. In either case she often got the same response from grown-ups that a parent gets from children. Yet underneath her position of superiority were feelings of inferiority which she tried to mask by acting parental as she had been forced to do when she was little.

Mr. Tenor's position was different. He was frequently touchy over imagined slights and often exploded over a chance word that hit one of his sore spots. Early in life his overanxious, overprotective mother had made him feel that he was not-OK. Nothing he did ever pleased her. So when he heard the people applauding for the folk-song group, he once again felt depressed—I'm not-OK, they are OK.

The psychological position that June Vague showed at the potluck was the hopeless attitude of one who sees no solution to a problem. This position can be *suicidal or schizoid. Early in life June's mother had frequently told her, "I almost died when you were born. I still suffer from your birth." As a little girl, June was unable to solve her mother's problem, and this failure was so unbearable that the feeling of futility permeated her life.*

Sally Walker's psychological position had been the exact opposite. Sally's behavior reflected her self-appreciation, her love of life, and her love of people. She felt OK about herself and, like Kathy and Raymond and Myra and Tom, she felt OK about others.

EGO STATE RESPONSES TO TRAGEDY IN THE CHURCH

Tom was feeling sad on the way to Sally's house. He was caught up in his grief surrounding her death. During the ten minute drive from the church office to her home he considered ways Sally's family might stand in need of his help. Their first reaction would be shock and disbelief. Once vibrant and alive, Sally was now dead, removed from their lives. What kind of support would they accept from him? Should he preach? Pray? Cry? Remain controlled? What?

Needing a little more time to control his own grief and to formulate a method of giving help to the parents, he pulled over to the side of the small dirt road. The aspen trees ahead still nodded. A few yellow wildflowers were still blooming on the hills. The white clouds floated across the sky, and in the quiet he could hear the sound of a dog barking and children playing. Tom had learned that his own spiritual needs had to be met if he was to meet the needs of others adequately. He took a deep breath, drank in the beauty and bowed his head. A scripture verse learned from his childhood came to mind, "I will lift up mine eyes unto the hills from whence cometh my help. My help cometh from the Lord which made heaven and earth."

Tom Hardy knew that some people, when faced with grief, wanted to hear the old beloved scripture phrases which had been "programmed" into their Child ego states. But Sally's mother did not have that programming. She had not had a church background as a child, so might very well be "turned off" if he used the traditional words of the church. If, for example, he were to say "It's all in God's hands," or "Let's pray about it," or "Put it all at the foot of the cross," he not only would fail to open a line of communication, but probably would offend her. Tom, using his Adult ego state to estimate probabilities, decided against the traditional approach.

What was he to do? How could he communicate concern through who he was rather than through what he said? Words would be insufficient unless he gave truly of himself. Tom decided he would listen and be available and sensitive to their needs to help them through their grief.

Such an approach would take time and energy, however, and setting new priorities for himself might become a problem. During the first couple of weeks he would probably have to spend less time preparing sermons, or skip his golf game, or delay some painting around the house that his wife had been wanting him to do for some time. She'd understand, but wouldn't like it very well.

Tragedy Compounded

Sally's mother met Tom Hardy at the door with a letter in her hand. After greeting him with understandable emotion, she handed him an envelope and said, "I just found this letter from Bob to Sally. It must have dropped out of his pocket when he came to get her. It hasn't even been opened. What shall I do with it? I can't bear to open it. Please will you see what it says for me?" Overcome with emotion she began to cry soundlessly.

Tom Hardy knew Bob as the intense, sensitive young man who was constantly around Sally, whose bright, warm personality made her a leader. As he opened the envelope he remembered Bob's fleeting, hurt expression when he had walked up to the birth-day table at the pot-luck supper. He unfolded a hand-written note:

"Sal—I've just about given up. I'm seventeen today and once more my Mom and Dad have forgotten that I even exist. What I thought was—if they were going to go out to another one of those damn cocktail parties, they might at least tell someone to have a birthday cake for me. But not a word all day. And now this evening—nothing as usual! Doesn't anybody care? What's the matter with me anyway? A long time ago I cut this clipping out of the church news-letter. It's where I'm at tonight. So I'm seventeen! So what?"

After reading the letter through twice, slowly, Tom turned to the poem[4] Bob had attached.

more than once
     I've missed a bus
  but one day
a chariot
        came swinging low
           even slow
and I missed that   too

Tom Hardy sadly handed both the note and the poem back to Sally's mother. Without words he waited quietly for her to read them. The seriousness of the accident was deeply compounded. Bob's choice of poems was almost prophetic. He had "missed the bus" once again when he had swerved his car—but at a tragic cost this time.

Briefly Tom's thoughts turned to Bob's immediate future. "Is Sally's death going to be one blow too many in his young life? Will Bob be in even worse shape than anyone else? Will his grief, guilt, and lack of parental caring push him into depression, even suicide?"

Tom began to turn over in his mind how he might establish the kind of relationship that might help free Bob from the sense of guilt. How could he interpret

Bob's situation to others so that in time Bob could experience reconciliation within himself, with Sally's parents, and with the community? Tom feared Sally's mother would be deeply resentful of Bob and assumed that this resentment would be too much to handle along with her grief.

He realized almost immediately that he was wrong. Sally's mother was aware of her feelings and not ashamed of them. For almost an hour she verbalized her rage against Bob interspersed with sobs and tears for Sally. At last the storm passed. Looking up at Tom she moaned, "What would my wonderful Sally want me to do?" Suddenly the expression on her face changed. "Oh, I know what she would want. She would want me to make it all right with Bob and with his parents. They must feel terrible now, just terrible. Poor Bob! Oh, Pastor Hardy, will you please bring him over here later when my husband gets back from . . ." The tears flowed again as she thought of the sad arrangements her husband was having to make, ". . . when he gets home. Please do it. Please."

Later, after bidding Sally's mother a temporary good-by, Tom was once more caught up in the sense of God's grace, of concern for others expressed in the middle of personal tragedy, of awareness of how much he could learn from Sally's mother, a woman who had never read a theological book, but simply knew how to love.

Tom contracted with himself to put acts of loving kindness toward others higher on his priority list. He might not be able to attend all the finance meetings. The painting at home might be delayed. Committee members and his wife might interpret this as a lack of love. Just maybe if he shared his struggle and concern they would understand.

A TA GOAL

Transactional Analysis is not only useful in understanding individual personality through the reality of

ego states. It is also useful whenever someone wants
to understand what's going on between people.

Common patterns of transacting with people are
often learned in childhood, copied from parents.
Sometimes the patterns interfere with communica-
tions of love. However, transactions can be analyzed.
If crossed or ulterior, they can be changed. They can
be made complementary, so that things get straightened out rather than remain "crossed up." This is a
redeeming experience that enables the church to be
more effective.

Psychological positions can also be analyzed and
relationships within a church can improve. Not-OK
feelings based on early childhood decisions can be
re-evaluated. New OK decisions can be made.

For this to happen, we need to give healthy, open,
complementary transactions high priority. We need
to trust the *Love* that was there in the beginning and
is here in the now.

EXERCISES IN RELEVANCY
(For Individual Use)

1. *Transactions in Sermons*

The effect of sermons is often unpredictable. The
message that is preached may or may not be accepted by the listeners. Consider a recent sermon
or lecture and ask:

- What seemed to be the ego state most often used
  by the speaker?
- To which ego state in me was the message sent?
- Were the transactions basically complementary?
  If not, what were they? Can I diagram one?
- Was there an ulterior message? If so, how was
  it conveyed?

2. *Responses to Praise and Criticism*

To discover some of the ways you respond to others:

- Write down three compliments you recently received.

- Next write down three criticisms you recently received.

- Now write down your response to each compliment.

- Next write down your response to each criticism.

Now look back at what you have written.

- Were there any ulterior messages sent? Any returned?
- If you crossed the transaction, how could you have responded differently?

3. The OK and Not-OK Positions

On the continuum below try to estimate the positions you usually have about yourself and about others.

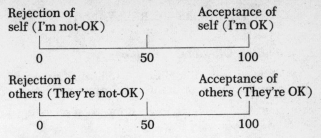

Think about yourself:

- Does your rejection and/or acceptance of yourself have to do with living up to some ideal? If so, is it realistic?
- Are you demanding too much or too little of yourself? If so, in what ways?
- Think of a few people close to you: Does your rejection or acceptance of them have to do with their living up to your standards? If so, are your standards realistic?
- Are you demanding too much or too little from them? If so, in what ways? Why are you doing it?

4. *Reliving Tragedy*

Many people have personally experienced tragedy in their lives. If you are one of them, go back in your memory and spend some time getting in touch emotionally with that tragedy. It will help you be sensitive to others.

5. *Resolving Priorities*

- Now think of some of the persons in the church who might be hurt, unhappy, alienated, hostile, or depressed.
- Think of yourself as "an agent of reconciliation.
- What might you do? Evaluate the possibility of your doing it.
- Decide what you are willing to do and when you will do it.

EXERCISES IN RELEVANCY
(For Group Use)

6. *Analyzing OK/Not-OK Positions*

After each person studies the following situations the group may wish to discuss the transactions.

Situation 1: An interfaith meeting to discuss open housing.

Father O'Malley: Our neighborhood is too homogeneous. It lacks a variety. We need to encourage people of other races to move out here.

Mr. Johnson: Yes, but we also need controls to protect our own property. If those people are allowed to move in the values will drop, and I worked hard for what I've got.

- From what position is Father O'Malley speaking?
- From what position is Mr. Johnson speaking?

Situation 2: In the pastor's study.

Joe Miles to Tom Hardy: I just can't seem to figure out how to put a worship service together. You've had so much better training than I have.

Tom Hardy: Maybe better training, maybe just more experience. I sometimes use a lectionary when I plan, but I enjoy hearing your own ideas, Joe.

- From what position is Joe speaking?
- From what position is Tom responding?

Situation 3: At a community mental health meeting.

Dr. Tripp: There are too many irrational cutbacks in funding and no one even asked people like us. We'll just have to give up this day care project for senior citizens. There's nothing to do.

Jessie Black: If it's really important we could volunteer our professional services. I heard of someone who tithed her time. As a social worker maybe I could do the same. That's 2 hours and 40 minutes a day. Would anyone else join me?

- From what position is Dr. Tripp speaking?
- From what position is Jessie Black speaking?

7. *Analyzing Transactions*

Now look at each of the above situations again.

- In Fig. 4.3, fill in the transactional stimulus and the transactional response in brief. Look for complementary, crossed, and ulterior transactions. These may change in the sentence, if so, draw additional sets of P-A-C circles until you think you have fully analyzed the dialogue.

8. *Transactions Here and Now*

- Draw a series of the P-A-C circles on the blackboard.

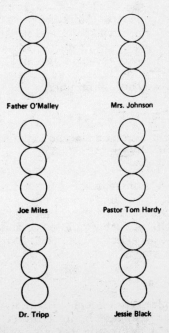

Father O'Malley   Mrs. Johnson

Joe Miles   Pastor Tom Hardy

Dr. Tripp   Jessie Black

Figure 4.3

- Let the group discuss the subject of transactions to clarify their thinking.
- Let the leader or other participants try to diagram the transactions as they occur in the class.
- If some of the transactions are crossed or have an ulterior dimension, do an "instant replay" to make the transactions complementary.

9. *Mass Media Transactions*

- Pass out a number of old magazines that participants have previously been asked to bring in.
- Suggest they flip through the advertisements to determine:
  1. What ego state is the ad writer trying to "hook" in the reader?
  2. What transactions are going on between persons in the ads? (You may have difficulty finding objective Adult pictures.)
- If there is time and space, and if paste and large sheets of paper are available, small groups can make collages of the ego states and of the various kinds of transactions. It's an entertaining activity that takes about 45 minutes.

10. *Church Budget Transactions*

To further understand transactions use the following statement: "We have a budget of _____ to meet this year."

- Make this statement three ways, from a Parent, an Adult and a Child ego state.
- After each statement let someone in the group respond from each of these ego states.
- Discuss how effective the original statements are and with whom.

11. *Transactions in Writing*

Many people have difficulty when writing. Sometimes because they are indirect or have a hidden agenda, sometimes because they are not sure of what they want to say, or do not have a "target" audience.

• Study the following memo:

To: Members of First Church
From: The Finance Committee

We know you are all concerned over the growth and mission of the church.

If we are to perform our mission adequately we must have more members who are willing to set aside a definite part of their income. If we grow in size of membership and size of financial commitment we will be able to expand our facilities.

Come to the parish meeting next week prepared to do your share.

• Now decide:
  1. From what ego state was it written?
  2. What ego state is it likely to "hook" in the reader?
  3. In what ways is it effective or ineffective? Why?

12. *T.L.C. in Tragedy*

The discussion of tragedy deserves considerable time. Therefore, an extra session, focusing on helpful transactions during crisis, would be more useful than trying to cover the entire chapter in one session.

• Start the discussion with the question, "If you were the pastor, deacon, relative, or neighbor, what might you do or say to Sally's mother and Bob and his family?"
• Why would you choose to say or do it?
• What does the church need to do when tragedy strikes?

13. *Helping Profession Panel*

In most churches there are professionals such as a physician, nurse, probation officer, school counselor, etc. who deal with people during crises.

• Arrange for a panel of such persons.
• Ask them to discuss what happens to people

physically, emotionally, and spiritually when faced with tragedy.

If the group is interested, visit institutions where people are troubled. Have a briefing session before visiting and follow the visit immediately with discussion.

YOU CAN
SEE GAMES
PEOPLE PLAY

CONFRONTING DEPRESSION

Two hours after his arrival at the Walkers' Tom Hardy was back in his car. "It was a pretty good start," he thought. "I deserve a gold stamp for being a better nurturing parent to Sally's mother than my father would have been. I used to think he could almost walk on water. Actually he was inadequate when he turned on his "preachy" voice and talked in pious phrases and told people how they should feel instead of respecting how they did feel. But now what to do about the Vague family?"

Pastor Hardy had known the Vagues for some time. He knew that Herb's mother had lived with them since the day Herb and June were married. Herb's mother was a real manipulator. When Herb came home from work, she would pull him down beside her on the sofa, pat his head and make comments such as "Now Herbie, tell me everything that happened in your office today," or "Now Herbie, you've had such a hard day. A man like you should rest. How about a cup of nice chicken soup?"

June and Herb used to argue about his mother. For years June had complained, "Something's got to be done with your mother, Herb. I just can't stand it any longer." Herb, with a hang-dog look, would typically respond, "Well, what can I do? After all, she's my mother."

Tom Hardy pulled up in front of the Vagues' home.

His knock on the door was answered by a worried-looking June. "Oh, it's you," she said. "Come in. Grandma's taking one of her little naps. I don't know how long it will last. I just never know what she's going to do."

Tom sat down, then broached the subject directly. "June, last night at the church supper I didn't have a chance to talk to you, but I'd like to now. Steve, down at the corner gas station, told me he saw grandma walking up the ramp to the freeway. He said she might have been killed, so he left the station and brought her home. Do you know about it, June? Is that why you're so worried?"

June sighed and looked away evasively. "I just don't know what to say. I didn't want anyone to know about it. You see . . . well, because . . ." June was floundering for an explanation.

"There just isn't anything we can do," she said. "Herb says he'd never forgive himself if he put his mother in a nursing home. It's true she wanders outdoors. Sometimes I think she's trying to get even." Her voice trailed off again.

Pastor Hardy broke in firmly, "June, it's time that you and Herb face the problem of his mother as it exists right now. She's no longer able to take care of herself. She needs to be taken care of."

June was barely listening to Pastor Hardy. "You know, there's something else I've been thinking about lately—off and on. . . . Well, I hate to bother you, you're so busy . . ." June began hesitantly.

Then she blurted in desperation, "I picked up a bottle of sleeping pills last week. I couldn't face all this any more." She began to sob uncontrollably. "I held those pills in my hand for a long time. I stood by the kitchen counter just hanging on to those pills. I couldn't take them, and I couldn't put them down. Maybe I'm the one who needs to be put away."

Pastor Hardy sat quietly by June and held her hand gently until she had stopped crying. Her serious depression and suicide threat indicated she might need extensive help. He asked, "Can you remember *any time in your childhood when you were overcome by similar feelings of being depressed?"*

June put her mind to the puzzle of her girlhood. "Well, I can remember thinking, I wasn't pretty. That my foot turned in. Another time I stuttered, and I had to wear winter underwear and no one else had to. Mother said I was always sickly. And she was always telling me how she almost died when I was born. I used to cringe inside and say, 'I'm sorry, it's too bad I was born.' Then she'd quickly explain, 'Oh, it's not your fault.' Besides that, my baby teeth had cavities and my father (who was a teacher) scolded me for that, and also for not learning to tell time fast enough.

"When I started school I used to throw up a lot, but I never told anyone. I didn't want to be kept home and be called sickly." June sighed deeply, "You know, Pastor Hardy, it even hurts to tell you about it." She saw the compassion and understanding in his eyes and burst into tears again.

A few minutes later, she looked up with a tentative smile and whispered, "What a relief to finally tell someone about it." Pastor Hardy took an envelope out of his pocket and, using it as he did his office blackboard, drew the three ego state circles, and began, "June, I want to introduce you to a system you can use to begin to understand why you feel so depressed at times. . . ."

Though June was distraught, she was nevertheless able to grasp some of the principles of transactional analysis. She learned how she had been programmed with messages in childhood that were still active in her Child ego state, and how she had decided on her "I'm not-OK" position. She also saw that she was still feeling and acting in response to those outdated messages.

Although Tom did not tell her this, he recognized June Vague as someone who needed more professional help than he would be able to give. He saw that she was probably acting out a self-destructive life drama with psychological "games" that furthered her script.

*June's final game payoff, if not changed, could end
in hospitalization or suicide.*

GAMES PEOPLE PLAY

June and Herb, like most people, played psychological games to reinforce their OK and not-OK positions about themselves and others.

All psychological games involve a series of transactions which are complementary on the surface.
Under the surface, however, there is always an
ulterior message. The ulterior message is the heart
of the game.

In some ways psychological games are like athletic
or card games. They have a series of predictable
moves based on stated or implied rules. It takes two
or more to play, and each player must know the rules
of the particular game. Like the athletic or card
variety, psychological games can be played at different
degrees of intensity, from a mild socially acceptable
level to a level of destruction of self or others.

A game begins with an invitation to play, which
is usually given indirectly—through a gesture, a look,
a word, etc. If the invitation gets a "yes" response,
either verbal or nonverbal, the game is on. It then
proceeds through a predictable set of moves and
usually ends with one or more players collecting a
particular feeling. This feeling is the payoff.

Games are learned in the family between the ages
of two and eight. Children either copy their parents,
imitating the moves their parents make, or they play
complementary moves which every game contains.
The moves in any game learned in childhood feel so
natural that few people are aware when they are
playing. Everyone has a repertoire of games and
spends a lot of time playing them. They are a familiar
way of relating to intimates, to coworkers and to
other people in general. The game formula is as
follows:

$$C + G = R \rightarrow S \rightarrow X \rightarrow P,$$

C = the con, the ulterior message Player 1 sends
to Player 2,

G = the gimmick, a weak spot in Player 2, such as
self-righteousness, sentimentality, criticalness,
cruelty, etc., that can be "hooked" by the con,

R = the response that Player 2 makes if hooked,

S = the switch, which is an unexpected next move
by Player 1 after Player 2 responds,

X = the confusion Player 2 experiences because of
the unexpected switch,

P = the payoff that each player receives.

JUNE AND HERB'S GAME

*For years June Vague had experienced feelings of
depression and futility. One of the games she played
to collect these feelings was If It Weren't For Them
(Herbert and his mother). She played this game at
the most intense third degree level from a basic
childhood position of I'm not-OK/You're not-OK. The
negative messages she had received from her mother,
such as "I almost died when you were born," had
left a disastrous imprint on June's Child ego state.*

One reason June played If It Weren't For Them

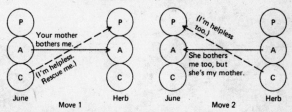

If It Weren't For Him (and His Mother.)

Move 1.	June acting the role of a victim, complains about her mother-in-law, expecting Herb to rescue her.
Move 2.	Herb responds by also acting helpless, inferring he is also a victim.
Continuing Moves:	Each indirectly asks the other for a rescue. Each refuses.
Payoff:	Turning away from each other feeling depressed.

**June and Herb's game (The broken lines are the
ulterior transaction, which is like a hidden message.)**

THE ALCOHOLIC PLAYS
HIS GAME—AND HIS WIFE PLAYS TOO

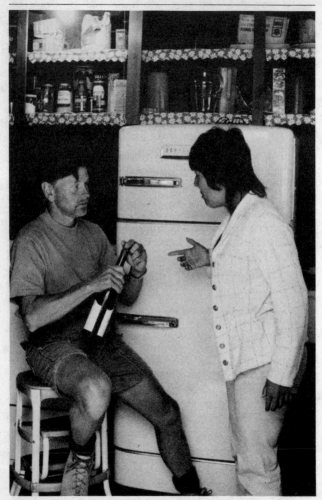

In the game of Alcoholic the drinker expects a hangover, a critical response from his spouse, and, eventually, forgiveness. The first move in the game is made when the person initiating it feels like a Victim, sorry for himself and in need of a drink.

The alcoholic continues to drink when he knows he's had more than enough and in spite of requests that he stop. Eventually a fight erupts. Each player expresses his or her resentments and frustrations.

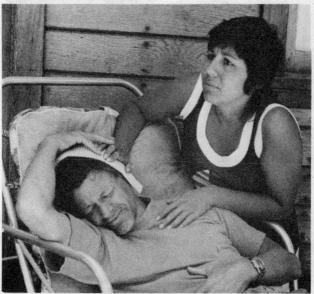

The fight ends when the initiator of the game first gets punished and later gets forgiven.

*was to avoid taking personal responsibility in relation
to her husband and to her mother-in-law. There were
a number of things she could have done. No one
forced her to play the martyr role. But by putting
blame on her husband she could maintain her original position of I'm not-OK/He's not-OK. (I'm not-OK
because I'm too weak or too confused to do anything
and He's not-OK because he won't do anything.)*

*June had learned to play this blaming game as a
little girl when she observed her mother playing it
with her father. Later in life she married the kind of
man with whom she could play the same game. Herb
had learned the same game as a little boy. His overly
indulgent and solicitous mother continually treated
him as a fragile child. He felt unable to escape her.*

GAMES PLAYED IN CHURCHES

Many leaders in the church are tempted to play
the game of *I'm Only Trying to Help You* when confronted by people such as June and Herb. Clergymen
who want to rescue others and who have a flair for
martyrdom in their script, play this game to support
their own position of I'm OK (being closer to God
because of my training) and You're not-OK (being a
sinner or uneducated layman who needs saving).
Such clergymen frequently keep people dependent
upon them.

One way an *I'm Only Trying to Help You* game is
initiated is when a parishioner brings a problem to
the pastor and asks for advice he really doesn't want.
Acting as nurturing parent the pastor is hooked into
the game. He tries to give advice (*Why don't you . . .*)
but all his suggestions are turned down (*Yes, but
that won't work because . . .*). The pastor may try
again to give advice, and again find it rejected with
"Yes, but. . . ." After several attempts to help are
countered with "Yes, but . . ." the pastor begins to feel
bewildered by the "ungrateful people" whom he "was
only trying to help."

This may reinforce his psychological position that
people are not-OK, that they are not grateful to those

who have the job of "saving" them. Conversely, the "Yes, but . . ." person who initiated the game in the first place gets his payoff by feeling gleeful. He has proven once more that no one can tell him what to do.

The same game is often played between a church school teacher and superintendent, or a women's circle member and a circle leader, or a choir director and a choir committee chairman, and so forth. A teacher may ask for help in lesson planning, then refuse all suggestions given; a circle member may do the same; a choir director may ask for suggestions for hymns or special music; a finance committee chairman may even ask for ideas on fund raising. Yet all "helpful" suggestions may be turned down with a "Yes, but . . ." and the problem remains unsolved.

A contrast to the *I'm Only Trying to Help You* player is the person who stores up feelings of hostility and resentment toward others and seeks opportunities to express those feelings. When he spots a real or imagined flaw, or catches others in a mistake, he plays *Now I've Got You, You S.O.B.* He feels justified in acting like a punitive parent and often does so with a *Now I've Got You* glint in his eye.

A committee can also play *Now I've Got You*. It may, for example, jump on a church member who has received a financial windfall, and by making him feel guilty, manipulate him into giving a large gift to the church (after all, he just bought a new car, house, clothes, etc. or took an expensive vacation). To compensate for his sense of guilt, the person who is pounced upon may either conform with a gift or may withdraw altogether from active church involvement.

Harried is another common game played by people who typically work hard, seldom take time off, erroneously believe that they are admired for their frantic schedule and aim to make others feel guilty for laughing, taking vacations and having fun. The payoff comes when the harried player collapses at a crucial moment and fails to achieve his goal, while moaning, "*Look How Hard I Tried.*"

The complaint "*Look How Hard I Tried*" is also

used by *Kick Me* players. However, instead of kicking themselves by playing *Harried*, they arrange for *others* to kick *them*. They may do this by being continually late, by doing poor work, by forgetting anniversaries, etc.

Churches can also play *Kick Me*. Innovations in the worship service or social action sermons can lead to getting kicked in some congregations. Infrequent church attendance, resistance to pledging, or refusal to teach a school class can also elicit kicks.

PSYCHOLOGICAL
TRADING STAMP THEORY

The most common payoff at the end of any game is the feeling a person "collects" for himself or gives to others. This feeling is colloquially called a psychological "trading stamp." Trading stamps are collected when emotions are "saved up" and not dealt with at the time these feelings arise. Some TA specialists assign colors to different feelings—blue for depression, green for envy, red for anger, or gold for the good feelings.

All young children feel. They feel "bad" when disapproved of, "mad" when treated unfairly, "depressed" when they cannot change an unhappy situation. For example, to frequent criticism with implied messages of "You're stupid," a child learns to act stupid, feel stupid, and collect feelings of "stupidity." Feeling stupid becomes his stamp collection. In response to frequent injunctions of "Aren't you ashamed of yourself?" a child learns that he is supposed to feel guilty. Guilt feelings become the basic stamp of his collection. Children also feel "good" when they receive approval, "glad" when treated fairly, "happy" when they discover their power to change some things. When grown a person keeps trying to collect the familar feeling stamps.

Stamp collections can be small or large, negative or positive. When a person saves up a small negative collection he may cash it in for a small prize such as a headache or an outburst of tears. If he saves up a larger collection he often feels justified in cashing it in for a larger prize, such as quitting a class or quitting a marriage or quitting society. The highest collector, like a big game hunter going in for the kill, seeks the bigest payoffs—suicide or homicide.

If a person saves up a small positive collection, he may cash it in for a small prize like some new clothes or an extra day off. If he saves up a larger collection he may cash it in for something like an exciting vacation or a new house. The most successful collector receives the best prizes—happiness, wholeness, and love.

TRADING STAMPS IN THE CHURCH

June Vague had learned early in her childhood to collect hurt and depressed feelings, one feeling at a time and one stamp at a time. She had saved a large collection of depression stamps and almost felt entitled to kill herself.

Her husband, Herb, saved the same kind of stamps but had not saved them with such intensity or for such a long period of time. Although his mother was a "smother mother," although he felt too weak to cut the psychological umbilical cord, and although he resented her power and his weakness, he frequently reminded himself, "At least I was wanted by my mother; poor June wasn't." Herb collected his prizes by dropping out of groups he would often join under June's persuasion.

Lisa, the church flirt with the beautiful solo voice and tantalizing figure, collected a gleeful prize in her game of Rapo whenever she was able to attract a man and then reject him, thus making him feel like a fool. Her childhood experiences influenced her basic position about men—namely, that they were fools who could be led on, then dropped. Although some wives resented Lisa's physical appearance and her invitational eyes, most of the men had caught on and recognized her game.

In contrast to June and Herb, Jean Pillar collected little feelings of frustration which sometimes built

The first move of Rapo is
made when someone hints
that she is sexually available.

Next comes the obvious response. The second player reaches for the bait.

The first player then switches the message, responding with "How dare you!" The second player is confused, and counters with "Gee, I didn't mean anything." The game ends with anger on the part of the woman, who decided in childhood that "You can't trust men," and frustration on the part of the man, who decided in childhood that "You never can tell what a woman wants." (The roles can be reversed, with the man initiating the game and the woman responding.)

up into anger. Jean usually cashed in her anger stamps a few at a time in small clashes with those with whom she worked in the church. This was what she was doing in her altercation with Mr. Pennyworth over juice and crackers and when she exploded in Pastor Hardy's study the morning after the supper.

Jean Pillar collected many of her anger stamps by playing her favorite game, Why Don't You. . . . She had played this game with Anne Green, the church school teacher, on the previous Sunday morning. Anne was putting the chairs in place after class when Jean walked in and looked at a pile of posters stacked on a table. Anne had sighed and said "I just can't get here early enough to put those posters on the wall, though I know the lesson would mean more to the children if I did. Oh dear!"

Anne's complaint had triggered Jean into her customary advice-giving role. First she suggested, "Why don't you come down on Saturday afternoon to do it." Next she offered, "Why not Saturday morning?" Then, "How about Friday evening?" Each of her "helpful" suggestions was met with "I have to take Mother shopping then," or "That's the time we do our laundry," or "That's the time of Mother's favorite TV program and she hates to be left alone to watch it."

With each of Anne's excuses Jean collected a red anger stamp, until she finally felt justified in cashing them in with the angry retort, "You'll never get anything done if you have to wait on your mother all the time. Why don't you stick up for your rights?"

Anne's response was "Yes, but no one wants to help me." Then Jean had the last word, "Well, Anne, I was only trying to help you!" This finished the game, and Jean collected a white stamp for purity and blamelessness.

Pastors, as well as parishioners like Jean Pillar, play games to collect stamps. Tom Hardy did so one Sunday morning when his alarm clock failed to go off promptly at seven. He collected another stamp when there was no coffee for breakfast because Betty had forgotten to buy it. When a Sunday School

Yes, But—

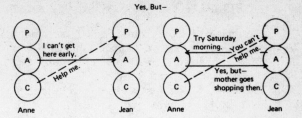

I'm Only Trying to Help You

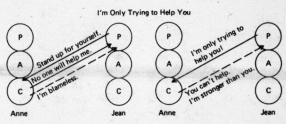

Move 1. (Anne presents a problem.) "I can't get here early enough."

Move 2. Jean offers a solution. "Try Saturday morning."

Move 3. (Anne has an excuse.) "Yes, but mother goes shopping then."

Continuing moves: Jean offers more suggestions. Anne has more excuses.

Move 4. (Frustrated by Anne's excuses, Jean retorts in anger.) "Stand up for yourself!"

Move 5. (Anne refuses to be blamed.) "No one will help me."

Move 6. (Jean's final move.) "I'm only trying to help you!"

Payoff: Anne reinforces a resentful Child position that no one can help her. Jean proves a Parent position that children won't try.

Anne and Jean's complementary games

teacher phoned in to tell him that he would need a substitute teacher for her class because she and her husband had decided to take an all-day ride in the country, Tom collected his third stamp. Hanging up the phone and feeling—but not voicing—increasing frustration, Tom added the last stamp to his collection when he noticed that some punch had been spilled on his new desk blotter. Ed, the custodian, unfortunately entered the office at that moment and

Tom cashed in his stamps by exploding into a game of Uproar.

"Ed, everywhere I look around here I see a mess! Why does something like this happen to me just when I need some last minute time on my sermon? Can't things ever go right around here?"

Tom Hardy regretted his accusation immediately and tried to stop the game. He knew his irritation was far more intense than the incidents of alarm clock, no coffee, missing teacher and spilled punch would justify. He also knew that Ed was a willing worker in spite of being slow.

Tom apologized, "A lot of things went wrong today, Ed, even before you came in. I'm sorry for taking it all out on you. It's really not all your fault."

Only partly mollified, Ed shuffled out to sweep up the rice and confetti on the front sidewalk. "If he'd just give me a chance, I'd a told him about what I come in for," *he muttered.* "Next time I'm going to complain about them late Saturday weddings. A man can't work 24 hours a day like I do!"

Ed was slow to feel resentment but before the month was out, he, like Tom Hardy, would feel entitled to his own explosion.

In one way Jean Pillar was very much like Ed. Both of them had a second brand of stamps they collected along with their angry feelings. These were stamps of blamelessness and self-righteousness. Each felt entitled to these purity stamps because each was always "trying so hard to help" people.

Feelings of self-righteousness are collected by many people in the church who have the position of I'm OK, You're not-OK. The church goer who is always on time and throws a disapproving glance at a late comer may be collecting a self-righteous stamp. Those who loudly sing all the verses of a hymn or repeat all the words of the prayers without looking in the books may also be self-righteous stamp collectors. Others may get stamps by making large donations where their names can be in print for all to see. Still others do the same by taking on more and more *church responsibilities. All feel and act like martyrs, thus collecting their purity stamps.*

Knowing the words of a hymn or a prayer, making donations, assuming responsibility for chairing a committee or for teaching in the church school are all worthy activities, but not when they are indulged in for the purpose of collecting stamps as a payoff—a prize at the end of a psychological game. Games fill time but detract from authentic living.

GAMES AND THE DRAMA TRIANGLE

People caught up in game playing are subconsciously using each game episode to prove over and over and over again their childhood positions of I'm OK or I'm not-OK and They're OK or They're not-OK. They play what are called the drama triangle roles, Victim, Persecutor, and Rescuer,[2] which they learned in childhood (see Fig. 5.1).

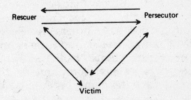

Fig. 5.1 The drama triangle

As children play house, cowboys and Indians, cops and robbers, doctor and nurse, they rehearse for future occupations and future games, acting as Victims, Persecutors, and Rescuers to each other. They try out the parts that fit the games they've observed their parents play and which they will play in more sophisticated ways in their own lives later.

As a game progresses, people switch roles. For example, an individual who plays a game from a Victim position using a script line such as "You never have my shirts ironed," or "You're always watching football," actually persecutes others. He tries to make them feel guilty. The switch in roles is obvious in the game of *Courtroom*. It is often played by couples who want to get out of the marriage or get even with their spouses. When they come for counseling, each acts like a Victim and insists that the spouse is the Persecutor. Each hopes to be rescued and hopes their spouse will be persecuted. In this game, as they explain the situation to the counselor from a Victim position, they also make persecuting statements to or about their spouse. If the spouse acts too disturbed by their accusations they may switch and become a Rescuer with a remark such as "Well, it really isn't that bad."

The counselor, if hooked into the game as a Rescuer, may also find himself playing the other roles. For example, if one player is dissatisfied with his "help" the counselor may feel like a Victim and respond as a Persecutor.

Some people play a basic game for each of the drama roles. As Victim, a person might play *See What You Made Me Do*, so that he can blame others. As Rescuer, he might play *I'm Only Trying to Help You*, so that he can save others. As Persecutor, he might enjoy playing *Blemish* and nit-picking the small blemishes or imperfections of others.

Everyone plays games from time to time. Many people have a favorite game because of their basic psychological position. For example, a man who expects misery may remain on the kind of job where he is sure to get it, may marry the kind of woman who will oblige him with more misery, and, if chairman of a church committee, will pick out people for his committee who will put him down. He would find it uncomfortable to work with a committee who didn't go along with his misery game, who were straightforward Adults, or who played a Pollyanna type game such as *Sunny Side Up*, that wouldn't fit his.

BREAKING UP A GAME

The quickest way to break up a game is to recognize it as such and to decide against playing the expected role. This decision can take place whether the game has been initiated by others or self-initiated. To recognize a game is to experience a flash of Adult awareness. It is not necessary to know the name of the game to break it up, only to recognize that a series of transactions with an ulterior purpose is going on and leading to a predictable payoff.

People who contract with themselves to look at themselves honestly and listen to criticisms with an open mind willingly admit that sometimes they initiate a game and sometimes they get hooked into a game initiated by someone else. For example, if a person realizes that he tends to initiate a Victim game of *Stupid*—doing and saying stupid things to reinforce his I'm not-OK Child ego state position—he can contract to stop his own game by thinking before he speaks and before he acts. By doing this he acts less like a Victim and more like the intelligent Adult he is free to be.

If a person realizes that he initiates *Blemish* or some other Persecutor type game, he can ask himself why he is doing it or why he places himself in a position to constantly criticize and if he likes the negative pay-off when healthy people avoid him. Churches or church members who behold the mote that is in their brother's eye and initiate a game of *Blemish* over it often need to consider the beam that is in their own eye.

If a person realizes that he initiates a game of *I'm Only Trying to Help You*, or some other Rescuer game, he can limit his rescuing time. If he's a professional, he can do his rescuing on the job instead of in his social life—except for emergencies, of course. He can also avoid overly-dependent people, and, when faced with a call for help, can ask himself something like, "If I don't jump in to rescue this person, will he be able to swim, float, or tread water to shore?" If he concludes that the person has this ability then the Rescuer can go about his own business.

If a game is initiated by someone else, one way to get out of it is to undermine the negative payoff. For example, if someone is playing *Kick Me*, and thus setting himself up for a psychological "kick," the second player can give a compliment or make a non-judgmental remark rather than furnish the expected "kick." This crossed transaction—an unexpected move which does not fit the game—interrupts the play.

Establishing distance is another effective technique for breaking up a game. A statement such as "I'll think that over," or "That's an interesting point, we'll discuss it at the next meeting," can be said in a manner that will interrupt players of *Blemish, Now I've Got You, You S.O.B.*, or *I'm Only Trying to Help You*.

An honest statement such as "I feel as if you want me to rescue you when you look sad," or "I don't like it when you phone me daily and talk for so long," can also break up a game. Briefly, to stop a game a person may:

1. Give an unexpected response.
2. Stop exaggerating his own weaknesses or strengths.
3. Stop exaggerating the weaknesses or strengths of others.
4. Give and receive positive strokes rather than negative strokes.
5. Structure more of his time with activities, fun, and intimacy.
6. Stop playing Rescuer, i.e., stop helping those who don't need help.
7. Stop playing Persecutor, i.e., stop criticizing those who don't need it.
8. Stop playing Victim, i.e., stop acting helpless or dependent when he's really able to stand on his own two feet.[3]

A TA GOAL

For people who are uncomfortable with others, or who do not like others, game playing is a way to avoid intimacy, a way to avoid responsibility, a way to avoid life and love, a way to avoid the pursuit of happiness.

TA shows what games are, the intensity at which they are played, and how to stop playing them.

Most people want to be open, honest, and authentic.

They fear, however, that they will not be accepted. They have forgotten, or never knew, that they were born for freedom and authenticity. People who admit to playing games can give them up—and replace them with honest, direct, reconciling relationships. They can experience the meaning of freedom because of the beginning *Love*.

EXERCISES IN RELEVANCY
(For Individual Use)

1. Responding to Trouble

Imagination is a valuable capacity we each have. With imagination we can design new ideas, structures, and relationships. We can plan the responses we'd like to have to daily transactions and crisis situations.

- Imagine you are the mother or father of Steve, the young man who works in the gas station and who found Herb's mother wandering up onto the freeway.
- Imagine you are also a long-time friend of June's, have known about her problems with her mother-in-law, but never discussed them with her.
- Imagine you have moved out of the community.
- Now imagine that your son, Steve, phones. He tells you how concerned he is over having found Grandma Vague near the freeway and pleads with you to do something about it.
- How would you feel? What would you say?
- How might each of your ego states respond?
- Which one would control you? Why?
- Now consider various options. Write them down.
- How could each option affect the relationship you have with June?
- How could each option affect the relationship you have with your son?

2. Feelings and Stamps

Get comfortable. Close your eyes and see yourself as the little boy or girl you once were.

- Go back in memory to an unpleasant childhood event. Stay with the memory to get in touch with the feelings you had then. (If you experience this feeling often it may have become your stamp.)
- Now go back in memory to some pleasant childhood event. Stay with the memory until you experience the same feeling you had then. (If you experienced this often, it could be your gold stamp.)
- Now try to remember how, when, and where you cashed in the feelings.
- In your current life do you sometimes have similar feelings? If so, with whom?
- Are the situations like replays of the early scenes? (If so, you may be collecting stamps.) How do you cash in your stamps currently?

3. Analyzing Games

Games involve two or more people. Everyone plays them from time to time.

- Review the games discussed in this chapter.
- Fill in the following, if they apply to you. List the person you play it with and the position from which you play it.

Name of the game	Played with	From the position of Victim, Persecutor, or Rescuer
If it Weren't for Him (Her)	_____	_____
Rapo	_____	_____
Why Don't You	_____	_____
Yes, But	_____	_____
I'm Only Trying to Help You	_____	_____
Uproar	_____	_____

Harried	_____	_____
Stupid	_____	_____
Kick Me	_____	_____
Blemish	_____	_____
Now I've Got You, You S.O.B.	_____	_____
Sunny Side Up	_____	_____

Another way to identify games is to use the following questions:

- What goes on between you and _____ that ends with one or the other of you having negative feelings?

- The game starts when _____ does (or doesn't) _____.

- The second move is by _____, who does

  _____.

- Next comes _____ by _____ , and so on.

- Finally the games concludes with _____ doing

  _____.

- The stamp collected for a payoff at the end of the game is _____.

4. *Stopping a Game*

Get in a relaxed position. Visualize yourself with someone who gives you bad feelings or who gets bad feelings from you.

- See what happens first.
- Then see what happens next.
- Last, see how it ends.
- Give the game a name.

Start an instant replay in your imagination and observe how and when different responses would stop the game.

5. *Facing Criticism*

(Although this exercise is designed for a church school teacher, it can be adapted to many situations.)

• Imagine that church school is out. Your pupils have left the classroom. The Superintendent comes in, walks over to you and hands you a letter from the Education Committee. The letter criticizes you or your department for:

(make this a possible realistic criticism.)
• How are you likely to respond outwardly to the superintendent?

• What goes on *inside* of you? In each of your ego states?

• What is likely to happen next?

• What psychological trading stamp would you collect?

• What game could develop to collect it?

• Try to diagram it and include a bit of the dialogue.

• Next imagine the same situation, but instead of a criticism you receive a compliment. Ask yourself the same questions as above.

EXERCISES IN RELEVANCY
(For Group Use)

6. *Stamp Collecting Situations*

Let each person study the following, then have open discussion.

Situation 1: A pastor, on short notice, tells the choir what hymns to sing. The choir had been planning to sing new music they had been rehearsing diligently.

- What feelings (stamps) might the pastor and choir collect?

- How might they cash them in?

Situation 2: One church member turns around and frowns at another who comes into worship late.

- What feelings (stamps) might each collect?

- How might they cash them in?

Situation 3: The youth group volunteers to tutor some younger children who are very obstreperous.

- What feelings (stamps) might each collect?

- How might they cash them in?

Situation 4: Select a current issue in your church and discuss what feelings could be collected and how they might be cashed in.

7. *Giving Stamps in a Group*

Before class session arrange to have cups with various colors of small simulated stamps made out of colored paper.

> Gold represents good feelings
> Green represents envy
> Red represents anger
> Blue represents depression
> White represents blamelessness—and so forth.

- Next, in small groups, discuss a current problem in your church, how it might be solved, and what procedure is needed.
- As participants talk, they may take and give a stamp to someone whenever they are in touch with their "good" or "bad" feelings. A brief statement as to the reason can accompany the stamp giving.

8. *Giving Up Games*

- Select a few of the games that were described in this chapter. Talk about them briefly.
- Then spend 15 minutes in small groups of two or three with the following assignment:

Each group will design and roleplay a simple game that might be played in a church.

After each game the same group will do an instant replay and break up the game.

YOU CAN REWRITE A PSYCHOLOGICAL SCRIPT

A BUSINESSMEN'S LUNCHEON

The last Friday of each month was the regular meeting of the Businessmen's Luncheon Group. Tom Hardy looked forward to this time he spent with other business and professional men in the community. He had become acquainted with members of the City Planning Commission, the Editor of the Weekly News, the Manager of First City Bank, and the Superintendent of Schools. All were concerned about community affairs; all used the luncheon to acquaint others with new programs or projects.

With so many pressures building up in the life of his church, Tom would have liked to skip this particular Friday meeting, but he was scheduled to present a new concept for community education and family counseling. Tom hoped to interest the businessmen, as well as his church, in the program and in providing some scholarships for needy persons.

As Tom hurried into the restaurant a few minutes late, he found the other men already gathered and about to be seated. Ernie Charles, a friend of many years, was there and in his good-natured way was shaking hands, thumping backs, joshing about golf scores with Father O'Malley, and generally creating a climate of good will. Tom wished Ernie would join the church, but whenever he broached the subject he

133

*was met with a friendly but firm refusal. Obviously
Ernie felt OK about himself, his family, his work as
a policeman, and about others.*

When studying scripts, Tom had once asked Ernie
about his childhood. He was interested in finding out
what experiences could have led Ernie to his OK
positions. Tom had been surprised at Ernie's response.
"I can remember getting praised a lot for imitating
the sounds of birds, animals, cars, and so forth—even
when I was in my playpen. Everyone thought I was
great, and I sure liked that. In fact, I still like it if
people think I'm great."

"If I could only get young parents to be as responsive
to their children as Ernie's parents must have been
to him," thought Tom as he waved a greeting, "they'd
all sure be happier. Maybe I could plan a course on
how to help kids become winners. I wonder."

Meanwhile, Joe Miles, the youth minister at First
Church, had arrived and was part of a group filling
up one of the farther tables. Joe was gregarious, like
Ernie. He saw a potential friend wherever he went
and often ended up agreeing to support their favorite
projects without quite knowing why. Though he was
not a member, he had a standing invitation to attend
the Luncheon Group whenever he could.

Only a few days ago Joe had lamented to Tom, "I
don't think I'll have time to go this week, I don't even
have enough time to prepare for my seminary
courses. I guess I get too involved with too many
people. I was trying to line up some summer jobs for
the high school kids, prepare a speech for the staff
of the Drug Center, and visit some kids in trouble at
Juvenile Hall. Then I got called by the drama club
to help them with their scenery and on top of that my
neighbor called me to help him pour some concrete!
And all this in one week! I don't seem to structure
my time well. What do you think I'm doing wrong?"

Tom had responded directly. "I think you're trying
too hard to live up to some image connected with
your name, 'Joe Miles.' You don't go one extra mile,

Joe, you go five. You're always trying to help and sometimes people really don't need it. I think you'd be more useful if you didn't always volunteer to carry everyone's problems on your back. Sometimes I think you must be living out some kind of superman or Atlas script."

"Atlas script?" Joe had queried.

"Yes, Atlas. Remember him? I got turned on to Atlas in an ancient history course. He was supposed to be a strong man in Greek mythology and carried the weight of the world on his shoulders because Zeus, king of the gods, made him do it for punishment. Later, when he didn't have to carry the world because Hercules could, Atlas chose to. Sometimes you remind me of him. You're so busy, so burdened, yet when someone offers to help you, you usually turn them down."

"Perhaps you're right." Joe gave a wry laugh. "Maybe that's exactly what I do. Then I get to feel like a full-blown martyr collecting self-righteous or purity stamps. Maybe I shouldn't act like a Rescuer when people don't need it. It probably keeps other people dependent on me. After all, if the world is saved it won't be by me. Like the good old Book says, it'll be because in the beginning was Love. Hmmm. I'll think about this."

Tom looked around the restaurant and noticed that another church member had entered, a man named J. L. Mark. His eyes were bloodshot and his face flushed. "As usual," thought Tom. "It must be really rough on him either at work or at home. I wonder what's going to happen to him."

Tom knew J. L. as a competent, hard-working salesman who sometimes drank too much and often spoke of himself negatively. Although he got along well with the men in the church, he had clashes with women on the finance committee. Once he'd told Tom that his dislike for women started when he was in the first grade. One day during a recess he and a friend had started fighting. J. L. won. No one was hurt, but just as the fight was finishing, the principal came by. She was a formidable, strong woman and dragged him into her office. She repeatedly hit J. L.'s knuckles with a ruler until they were bruised and bleeding. He decided on that day that even if he'd won the fight, he was really a loser. Three years later, when his mother died of pneumonia and a series of housekeepers took over, he was even more sure of it. Especially when he was criticized with "No wonder your poor mother died. The way you act would drive anyone to the grave!"

Tom was thinking about this as he walked over to J. L. He wondered if these childhood experiences had been so painful that J. L.'s dislike of women would be disruptive again at the committee meeting scheduled for that evening. The opportunity to talk the whole thing over hadn't occurred, but "Maybe," thought Tom to himself, "just maybe I'm just using that as an excuse to avoid being direct, to avoid what might turn out to be unpleasant or time consuming or something I don't want to face."

Tom's directness to Joe and Ernie was possible because he felt comfortable in his relationships with them. It was also an outgrowth of his interest in TA and his study on psychological scripts. In the training seminar Tom had attended, considerable emphasis had been placed on scripts and Tom had felt very excited as he discovered the two sets of stories that he had unknowingly been following—the Hardy Boys series and the story of Doubting Thomas. Script prototypes are often found in myths, fairy tales, and children's stories. He knew that Berne believed that "Sooner or later a child hears a childhood story or fairy tale about 'someone like me,' and that tells him what he is headed for."[1] Tom's script, like these of Joe, Ernie, and J. L., was a life drama about which he had only partial awareness. Each felt compelled to behave in certain ways, thinking and acting as though following stage directions and reading lines written by someone else.

INTRODUCTION TO SCRIPT THEORY

A *script* can be briefly described as a *life plan*, very much like a dramatic stage production that an individual feels compelled to play out.

A life plan is based on the early decisions and positions taken by a child and "reinforced by the parents, justified by subsequent events, and culminating in a chosen alternative."[2] Because the script is in the Child ego state, it is "written" through transactions between the child and his parents. The psychological games played are small scenes that are part of the script. This life plan, this script, is usually selected before the age of six and although a person is not aware of it, he or she compulsively plays the parts. Like a theatrical play, a psychological drama has a theme. The most common themes are "love, hate, revenge, or jealousy."[3] Scripts can be classified as constructive, destructive (to self and/or to others), or going nowhere.

A person with a constructive script cares about the world and its people, values them as well as self. He or she achieves some measure of "greatness," though it may never be written about in book or newspaper. Fame is not the criterion. Whether known or unknown, the person with a constructive script leaves the world somewhat better for his having been a part of it. He not only cares about his own health and happiness, he cares about that of others. He actively works against situations that contribute to poverty, disease, discrimination, and other problems that lead to other people's unhealthiness and unhappiness.

A person with a destructive script sooner or later injures himself and/or others. He or she may do this gradually and over an extended period of time or suddenly, in a dramatic fashion. If a person is destructive of self, he may, for example, drink, eat, or work himself to death, drive like a fool, crash his car, or commit suicide in an even more obvious manner. If a person is destructive of others, he will destroy or hurt them, either physically or psychologically. His attitude may also be one of indifference

The do's and do not's,
should's and should not's of
giving and receiving affection
also become part of a script.

toward the suffering of the world. Without a sense of guilt he will allow, or even encourage, the maiming, killing, and starving of helpless victims of political machines.

A person with a going-nowhere script restricts his own growth, limits his own opportunities, and avoids the full realization of his potentials. This person often follows the stereotype expectations of the larger culture. On the surface he may appear successful, as though he has a constructive script, but inevitably he undermines himself in some way and explains his misfortunes as bad luck. In other words, when the curtain is up the person may be oriented toward useful activities, yet when the final curtain comes down, nothing really important has been accomplished. This is the script of many people who say "I tried." These people aren't really going anywhere. They're too busy trying instead of doing and being.

Along with their scripts, many people have what is called a *counterscript*. This is a "possible" life plan in their Parent ego state that may be in opposition to the script in their Child.

Counterscripts occur because many people receive non-verbal negative script injunctions from their parents, and also receive verbal and positive messages from them that go counter to the script negatives. Counterscripts are formed by the (usually positive) mottos or useful moralisms passed through the generations from Parent ego state to Parent ego state. They include culturally acceptable statements such as: "Laugh, and the world laughs with you; weep, and you weep alone," "If at first you don't succeed, try, try, again," "There's no use crying over spilt milk," "A stitch in time saves nine." It's interesting that so many folk sayings are directly contradictory; e.g., "Look before you leap," and "He who hesitates is lost."

When the script and counterscript messages are positive as well as congruent, the person usually has a constructive script.

Whereas the script in the Child directs a person's fate and the counterscript in the Parent determines the lifestyle, the Adult ego state can autonomously decide what to keep and what to discard of each.

The development of the Adult ego state to deal with objective reality by data processing is aided if a person's parents used their own Adult ego states to demonstrate "Here's how to do it." For example, a parent may say, "Here's a dictionary and here's how to use it," or "Here's a hammer and here's how to use it," or "Here's a needle and thread and here's how to use it." This Adult "Here's how" is not part of the script because the script, by definition, is in the Child ego state.

Transactional analysis is a potent "Here's How" tool for the person who, from his Adult, decides in favor of autonomy and who sticks by the decision.

THREE SCRIPTS IN FIRST CHURCH

Tom Hardy

Tom's names received special attention when he was little. Many children are given names of biblical or storybook characters, national or family heroes, movie stars, and so forth, and are expected to copy their namesake. Tom Hardy was one of these.

As a boy he was unusually healthy. He so seldom caught colds that his father used to brag about it. "You really are a hardy one." This was reinforced by his physician grandfather who declared, "Doctors are for sick people. Now think about that. You don't need to be sick."

When Tom was in the sixth grade, his favorite books were the Hardy Boys series, and he became deeply involved in their detective-like abilities to solve mysteries. He also spent long hours with jigsaw and crossword puzzles, encouraged by his mother.

Tom's first name had also received attention. As a bright adolescent who had to attend church regularly, Tom occasionally argued with his father over some of the points made in his father's sermons. Tom's father, from his theological corner, would respond indulgently with, "You're just like your namesake, Thomas. He doubted everything. Someday you'll figure out the mysteries of faith for yourself. Just keep thinking."

This interpretation of his name was a scripting message for Tom because the family joke of identifying Tom with "Doubting Thomas" implied that he would have a questioning attitude and insist on proof, even as a young child.

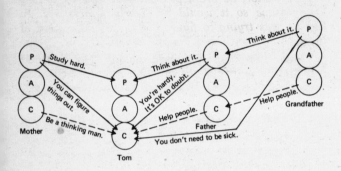

Tom Hardy's original childhood scripting
(The broken lines are the constructive, nonverbal
messages. The solid lines are the verbal directions.)

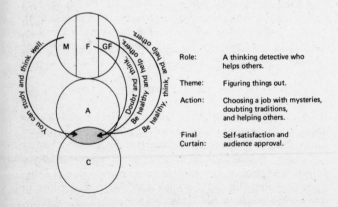

Role:	A thinking detective who helps others.
Theme:	Figuring things out.
Action:	Choosing a job with mysteries, doubting traditions, and helping others.
Final Curtain:	Self-satisfaction and audience approval.

**Tom Hardy's constructive script in action in
later life** (The inner dialogues are like stage directions
to advance the script. If a person is not aware when
he is in his script, his adult is contaminated by it.)

In a number of ways the Hardy Boy roles were compatible with the biblical Doubting Thomas, so as he was growing up, Tom continued to doubt, question, and try to puzzle out the mysteries of existence.

As a pastor, he often puzzled over how to convey his message so it would be clearly understood. In fact he was trying to figure out the biblical story of the Good Samaritan from the standpoint of Transactional Analysis. In his pocket at the luncheon was a preliminary outline[4] for a sermon that read:

Traveler: *I'm not OK—you're OK! Traveler's script called for getting hurt!*

Priest and Levite: *I'm OK—You're not OK! Position of many religious folk.*

Robbers: *I'm not OK—You're not OK. A Cops and Robbers game!*

Good Samaritan: *I'm OK—You're OK! The Prince!*

Austin Tenor

Austin's Tenor's family came to America before he was born. To his parents, America was a place where hard work might mean success and acceptance. Both mother and father worked in a grocery store long hours and, although they encouraged Austin to study music, they showed little interest in his progress. When Austin was in a recital they were always "too busy" to go. When he won a musical award in high school, they suggested he change his interests. According to his mother, he'd "never make a good living at music like his brother Ben would by selling real estate." According to his father, "It's not good to be too good. Someone might notice and begin to ask questions."

Austin's father was a frightened man. As he had not filed for citizenship papers he was afraid of being caught, questioned, and deported. He often cautioned Austin, "Walk quietly in the shadows and don't make any noise."

Actually Austin was very talented, had received

good training, and was capable of a successful pro-
fessional career. However, his scripting messages
from his parents had strongly implied "Don't succeed
financially," and "Don't be well known." Austin com-
plied with the message by working long hours in a
men's store, six days a week, using his talent only
briefly on rehearsal night and in the Sunday worship
service.

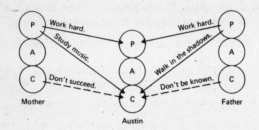

Austin Tenor's childhood scripting
(The broken lines are the don't-succeed, go-
nowhere messages. Usually they are nonverbal
but they can have verbal reinforcement.)

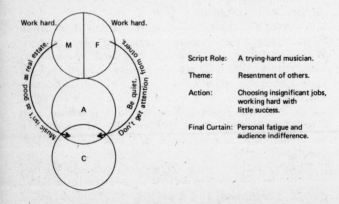

Script Role:	A trying-hard musician.
Theme:	Resentment of others.
Action:	Choosing insignificant jobs, working hard with little success.
Final Curtain:	Personal fatigue and audience indifference.

Austin Tenor's going-nowhere script
in action (The inner dialogue heard by Austin
contaminates his adult performance.)

Whereas Tom's script theme was constructive and that of a winner, Austin's theme was of going-nowhere. He was a nonwinner, one who neither wins nor loses but just manages to stay even. His script contaminated his Adult thinking and behavior.

June Vague

June's script was even worse than Austin's. She was scripted to be an out-and-out loser because she had been told repeatedly that her birth caused her mother's ill health and emotional breakdown. She collected hurt and depressed stamps by playing If it Weren't for Him (and his mother) and Kick Me. She blamed others for her miseries and often whined like an unhappy four-year-old to get her kicks from them. Like Lisa, she was unable to see what she did to collect her stamps. Unlike Lisa, who was out to make men feel foolish, June was out to destroy herself because she did not feel entitled to be alive. This was an old feeling from her childhood.

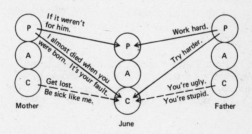

June Vague's childhood scripting (The broken lines are the nonverbal destructive messages.)

In June's marriage to Herbert she often replayed her childhood scenes. When around her husband, she felt as stupid and inadequate as she had when around her father. When near Herbert's mother she often felt as depressed and guilty as she had when she was around her mother.

These negative feelings were so strong that June, when in her Child ego state, actually believed that if she just tried harder, as her father had continuously told her to do, Herb and his mother would give her approval.

However, when June shifted into her Parent ego state, which is very common when the inner child is hurting, she acted quite differently. Sometimes she acted like her mother and made others feel guilty; other times like her father, admonishing others to "try harder."

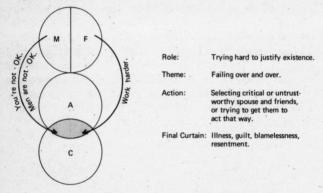

Role:	Trying hard to justify existence.
Theme:	Failing over and over.
Action:	Selecting critical or untrustworthy spouse and friends, or trying to get them to act that way.
Final Curtain:	Illness, guilt, blamelessness, resentment.

June Vague's destructive script in action
(June spends years working and "trying hard" with Herb and his mother while playing the same games her own mother played when June was little.)

THE SCRIPTING BEGINS

The scripting begins and the final outcome of a life drama is sometimes determined in the womb or soon after birth. If pregnancy is wanted, if the genes of both parents are satisfactory, if the physical and emotional condition of the mother is healthy and the event of birth normal, then a child is likely to begin life feeling OK.

If a child is cared for properly in the early months of his existence, and if he receives positive attention, both emotional and physical, from those around him, he is likely to continue feeling OK. Over the years, this gives him permission and encouragement to *be himself*, to explore and to think for himself; he is likely to have an I'm OK, you're OK script, and consequently love himself, love others, and love living.

On the other hand, if a child is not wanted, if something goes wrong during pregnancy or at birth, if he is "just one more mouth to feed," or "just one more baby to diaper," if his parents frequently feel resentful, frustrated, or angry at his being alive and being their responsibility, a child is likely to have an I'm not-OK, you're not-OK script and dislike himself, dislike others, and dislike living.

Often children get mixed messages and conclude they are partly OK and partly not. Instead of unconditional love in the beginning, they receive conditional love. Conditional love is "if" love. It is the kind that is given *if* you keep your dress clean, *if* you don't make any noise, *if* you get good grades, *if* you do what you're told to do and comply with other people's demands.

Children who are scripted with conditional love are often high in performance but low in self-esteem. They often feel as though nothing they do is good enough. They try and try, but never quite succeed. They fluctuate between the two positions: I'm OK, you're not-OK, and I'm not-OK, you're OK. They go around and around similar tracks and never break out into the open where they could stand a chance of winning.

According to script theory, people compulsively—but with little awareness—play out the drama of their lives in ways that resemble their childhood scenes. In childhood they make decisions about themselves that are based on these scenes. Next, their decisions are crystalized into logical positions. On the basis of this process each child adopts a script behavior before the age of eight, usually a myth, fairy tale, or children's story to identify with and act out. The process is diagrammed as:

| Childhood experiences | → | Childhood decisions | → | Psychological positions | → | Scripty behavior |

The loving affection and
intelligent care of a mother
contributes to a child's sense
of worth and self-esteem
and leads the child toward
a constructive script.

The loving touch of a father
is also vitally important
for healthy development.
So many homes are
currently without fathers
that churches need to
develop substitute-father
programs in order that the
children involved may be
spared the deprivation
that may occur if they are
totally without grownup
male companionship.

For example, a child who experiences brutal parents is likely to decide that it is safer to stay away from grown-ups; that they are not-OK. He may also decide not to grow up and select a Peter Pan script. Then he will unknowingly look for a mother type, like Wendy; for someone to drink the poison intended for him, like Tinker Bell; for boys to play with and others to fight against as in the story. Finally he will look for a Captain Hook, to be as cruel as his own parents were.

In real life Peter Pan can be a girl as well as a boy and Captain Hook a "witchy" woman as well as a cruel man. The point is that the central character chooses a land of child fantasy instead of growing up.

THE SHOW ON STAGE

The script written in childhood is rewritten during adolescence—often at a more sophisticated level than it is rehearsed. The show goes on stage when a person is in their early twenties.

Each person has his own drama, and each tries to direct his own show, either overtly or covertly, as well as be on stage. As director, each looks for others to play certain roles in a particular way. This is like selecting members for a theatrical cast.

The process is similar to baiting a hook for a particular fish. The bait is colloquially called a "sweatshirt." A sweatshirt carries a message sent from the Child ego state to attract another player or to keep one away. Like a costume, the sweatshirt hints at what's to come (for example, Tom Hardy's sweatshirt message was "Lean on me"). Whatever the message, if it looks appealing to the Child of another person, he may swallow the bait. Thus, the action starts and moves from scene to scene or game to game.

The selection process is important to the outcome of the game, for when two people are sharing the same stage their dramas might fit together or they might not. For example, if a woman had a Peter Pan script and her husband had one of Robinson Crusoe, their scripts would not be complementary. When on stage together, their drama would be disjointed. The stage "director" in each one of them would try to control the other, but the characters wouldn't quite fit together. On the other hand, a woman who has a Wendy role in a Peter Pan script may select a husband with a compatible script who will go flying off like a little boy. She may go home to her parents or find another Peter Pan.

The drama may be funny or tragic, dull or exciting, melodrama or pilgrimage, but at last the final curtain falls, the audience responds, and the players get their final payoff.

Berne has observed that "scripts are only possible because people don't know what they are doing to themselves and to others."[5] A person in his script is like someone at a player piano, acting as though the music is his creation, and sometimes rising "to take a bow or a boo from his friends and relatives, who also believe he is playing his own tune."[6] In each life script there is a repetition compulsion. The acts that people play out when grown, and the characters they select for their stage, are often repetitious of childhood scenes and characters.

When people get married they have three TA contracts: (1) a legal contract with a marriage license, Adult to Adult, (2) a relationship contract, most frequently Parent and Child, in which each expects to take care of, and be taken care of, in particular ways, and (3) the script contract in which each plays certain parts and expects the other to do likewise Child to Child. One of the most common expectancies for a woman is that her husband will act like her father; for a man, it's that his wife will act like his mother. Both husband and wife try to give an invisible script, with dialogue and actions, to the other—and they try even harder to direct how the show should go.

Occasionally the course of a drama changes. For example, in a marriage of many years, if one or the other gets tired of the same old act, refuses to play the expected role, and insists on change, the marriage drama changes accordingly. Conflict may emerge, the cast may separate and each move to other stages

PLAY IS OFTEN A SCRIPT REHEARSAL

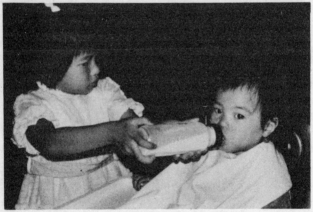

The way children spend their free time,
having adventures, playing school or house, etc., is
often a rehearsal for what they will do in later
life; the roles they play are basic script roles. For
example, children on a raft may play at being Victims
who are castaways or who need to escape. Or they
may play at being Persecutors and attack a common
enemy—or each other if things go rough. Or a
child may play at being a nurturing Parent. All these
roles may be similar to those they will play later, when
they are confronted with real-life situations.

and other shows—shows that, unless they are carefully worked at, may be strangely similar to the old one (see Fig. 6.1).

Life is never hopeless, however; changes made on the basis of script awareness can be very constructive.

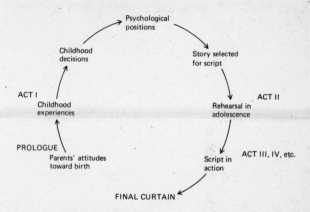

Fig. 6.1 The drama repeats itself
(Each new act contains replays of previous acts,
though sometimes with new scenery and characters.)

SCRIPT AWARENESS

The script a person lives by is the life plan he has chosen to enable him to reach his final goal in life. Each person is at least partly aware of this compulsion that forces him to his destiny. Since the psychological drama is originally directed by parents, many of the details as well as the goal can be predicted.[7]

To become aware of some of the elements of one's script is the first step in changing it. If a person is unaware, his Adult is unknowingly contaminated. Awareness gives power to the Adult. A person who is alert to being in his script can suddenly stop the play acting of his inner Child—who may expect something magical to happen—or he can stop inappropriate

negative feelings, thoughts, and behavior that can
lead to an unhappy ending. A person who is aware
of the script can get a better "show on the road" if
he decides to do so. In the process of becoming aware
and making new decisions the ego state boundaries
are realigned. The clear thinking Adult becomes the
executive of the personality and directs the new
action (Fig. 6.2).

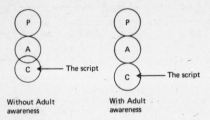

Fig. 6.2 Ego boundaries and script awareness

Script awareness can be achieved in several ways.
One way is for a person to *listen* to his internal
dialogue, the shoulds and should nots, the musts and
must nots of his parent figures; also the pleadings,
manipulations, and excuses of his Child ego state.
*With script awareness a person can choose to go
against any inner dialogue parental directives that
are destructive or that no longer make sense to him.*

Another way to script awareness is for a person to
look at his life drama as though watching a movie;
to see once more the things he wanted and the early
parent-child transactions that influenced his script so
that he could—or couldn't—get what he wanted. This
replay of earlier scenes can be helped by a journey
through a childhood photograph album. Looking
closely at the people and the background often opens
closed doors in one's memory.

A third way to script awareness is to recall one's
favorite myth, fairy tale, or children's hero story. It
usually reveals the roles, theme, action, and finale
that have been chosen for a life drama. If a person
can't remember what his favorite story was, a family

member who read to him as a child, or who listened to the same radio or T.V. shows with him, may be able to help the recall.

Another way to awarenes is ask key questions. For example, asking oneself "What would other people write for my tombstone if I died today?" is one way of discovering what the "audience response" might be. Asking oneself "If I were to write my own epitaph, what would I say?" is a way of discovering what role is being played and whether the role fits the reality known by the Adult.

Although each person identifies with one particular role, most often the Victim or Rescuer, he will know and be able to play all the roles of his favorite story, including the role of Persecutor. (When the words Victim, Rescuer, and Persecutor are capitalized, they refer to script roles, otherwise they refer to legitimate positions.)

Script awareness includes an understanding of these drama roles. One person may be play-acting a role if he asks "Why are you picking on me?" while looking like a Victim with a hurt expression on his face. The same person may be playing the role of a Rescuer if to one who looks downcast, he gives a sympathetic look and asks, "Can I get you a cup of coffee or an aspirin to make you feel better?" He also plays the role of a Persecutor if, with a stern look, he implies that a rule has been broken when he finds someone sitting in his favorite chair or reading the morning newspaper ahead of him.

In some people these roles are characteristic ways of behaving. They were learned in childhood, feel familiar inside the person's psyche, and fit into his script.

Of course not all victims, rescuers, and persecutors are roles played from the Child. Sometimes they are real and are related to actual here-and-now situations. For example, people who are actually discriminated against because of race, sex, age, or national origin are real victims, not play-acting ones. People who see others actually suffering and try to do something to relieve that suffering are real rescuers, not compulsive role-playing ones. People who are judge or jury in a

law court may be legitimate persecutors and not playing the part.[8]

Script awareness involves knowing when, where,
how, and with whom the basic drama roles are played.
It also involves knowing how the roles fit the drama
and what is likely to happen next. Script awareness
involves remembering parental do's and don't's, both
verbal and nonverbal, that came from each ego state
of each parent. These may have been in conflict or
they may have been in harmony. If in harmony, a
person will feel "together" with himself.

PEOPLE OF THE BOOK

Historically people in the church have often been
called the "People of the Book." They turned to the
Bible as the "word of God," read and listened to the
timeless messages, argued and prayed over the possible meanings.

Often their ego states have had conflicting views
of the scriptures, and so crossed transactions have
occurred and psychological games have been played.
In spite of this, a "Christian" script based on biblical
tradition has been an important theme in the lives of
many people. It was like this for Joe Miles, who was
scripted to go the "second mile," and for Tom Hardy,
with his Doubting Thomas part.

Although church members have been considered to
be "People of the Book," fewer of them are reading
the Book and fewer and fewer are involved in any
religious studies.

One reason may be because so many other books
are now available. In previous generations, the Bible
was the only book (or one of very few books) in many
homes. But now millions of books, and radio and T.V.
programs as well, compete for people's attention.

Another reason may be that in previous generations
the pastor and the Book were often accepted as "the
authorities" in society. This is no longer true. There
is a wide segment of society that seems to be against
authority in any form. Because the Bible has so often
been used in an authoritarian manner, to elicit feelings of shame and guilt, some people erroneously

equate authority with authoritarianism and discard the Bible as being irrelevant.

A third reason might be the unwillingness or inability of some churches to provide adequate adult education in biblical history and literature, as well as in theological interpretation. Unfortunately the emphasis in too many churches has been placed on sentimental Child or legalistic Parental interpretations.

A fourth reason for ignoring the Book could be the "scripting" many people have had about books in general and about their personal abilities to study.

BIBLE READING IN FIRST CHURCH

In First Church, as anywhere else, people were scripted differently for reading and studying. For example, Joe Miles had considerable inner conflict with his studying. Neither of his parents read much, although both were very active in helping others. His father was a scout executive and his mother a leader at church and in the P.T.A. When Joe sat down to his seminary studying, he often felt an inner nudge and heard the words "Go out and get something done and don't just sit around all day reading." Joe was in a bind. He felt guilty if he read the Bible, and guilty if he didn't. When preparing a sermon he often practiced reading the scriptures aloud, but felt silly when doing so.

Suzanne was different. She enjoyed reading as a little girl and both of her parents read widely. Therefore a positive attitude toward reading was in her Parent and Child ego states. However, during her adolescence Suzanne resented the academic world of her parents and stopped studying for some years. Later in life her Adult decided in favor of reading. This put her three ego states in accord. Suzanne returned to school, received honors, and learned to enjoy people from both the academic and nonacademic worlds. She also became excited over the Bible, which she read for the first time in seminary.

J. L. Mark's reading patterns were more erratic.

His father had been a high school and Sunday school teacher whom J. L. "could never please, no matter what." If J. L. received a good "B" grade in school, his father demanded an explanation: "Damn it, why didn't you get an A!" J. L.'s mother spent several hours each day escaping into movie and "confession" magazines which she tried to hide each evening before Mr. Mark came home. Consequently J. L. fluctuated between reading trash and reading what might please his father. In the Bible study class when they were reading Genesis, J. L. became critical of the two different stories of creation and exploded, "Why isn't the Bible better organized! I never did understand why they call it the 'good' book. Furthermore, I don't like the idea that somebody up there will take responsibility for me or has the answer for me. That's the way my own father acted and I don't like that one bit."

Few people know all the Bible, many know parts of it, and tend to emphasize only those parts that uniquely fit what they want to believe. Although the Bible offers a variety of script themes as well as the promise of freedom, if people don't read it they are not aware of its many options.

REWRITING THE SCRIPT

The challenge to rewrite a script, or any part of a script, comes *after* awareness of the script itself. Then a person has three choices: (1) to stay in it, (2) to stay out of it, (3) to rewrite it. The first is easy; the last two are hard and take work and energy.

If a person decides to play out his life *in* his script, he will try to justify his decision with arguments, to himself or another, such as: "Yes, but, someday . . .," or "There's no escape for me. Nothing can ever change . . .," or "I'm so stupid I just don't know how to . . .," or "No matter what happens life will always. . . ."

If a person decides to stay *out* of his script, he will try, often desperately, to turn off the inner Parent-Child dialogue and suppress his Child ego state, where the scripting is lodged. This requires constant vigilance, because whenever the Child is triggered off there is a strong possibility of "flipping into the script." This is a frequent occurrence, because the Parent ego state often carries on running commentaries about everything. The Child listens unknowingly and is also activated by many external stimuli. To stay aware of both ego states and to fight against contamination of the Adult by both the Parent and the Child is to be always on guard—and that takes a lot of work and energy.

Therefore, to rewrite a script, which is the third and best choice, is to have more options and ultimately less pressure. Rewriting a script requires an awareness of what the script originally was and how it was given. It also requires an awareness of how the script is currently being played out and whether there is a counterscript and how it is operating. Professional help from a therapist may be necessary to discover it.

Then comes the most important step—the crucial decision to finish off the act, "bring down the curtain," and re-write subsequent scenes. Bringing down the curtain means to put a stop to the destructive or going-nowhere feelings and behavior. It means to become an Adult stage director who says to the Child, "Knock that off. You don't have to do that. Be real instead."

To be real is to feel and act from your Child ego state, to feel and act from your Adult ego state, and to feel and act from your Parent ego state—all at the appropriate times and in the appropriate places.

Being real instead of playing a role will call for new ways of responding, both verbally and nonverbally. It calls for tolerance instead of intolerance, honesty instead of artificiality, loving instead of "getting even," involvement instead of withdrawal. It will require awareness, decision, and follow-through.

The rewriting may include a change of characters, scenery, dialogue, and so forth. However, the redecision of the main character is the turning point. The redecision often includes going against the inner Parent who has been directing the Child in its show and enlisting a new director, the Adult. The Adult, as director, can work with the Child, as main character, and together they can change the script. For example, if the script is moving toward an unhappy ending they can add or delete what is necessary to make it happy.

Family members, friends, teachers, or professional therapists may assist in the becoming-aware process. They can even suggest specific ways of changing. But ultimately it is up to the individual person to rewrite his own life drama.

A TA GOAL

Everyone makes their own life plans. Early in childhood everyone chooses how to live, how to die, and what to do with their time in between.

People who become aware of their scripts and choose to stay in them are people of little faith, they do not trust their own power to live a real life.

Life is what happens between birth and death, life with its challenge, its loneliness, and its love. The way you are scripted to live it, cope with it, give and receive it, is your drama. If your drama is destructive, either to yourself or others, or if it is going nowhere like a treadmill, you can rewrite it and put a better show on the road. You can be a real person; you can be spontaneous, rational, and trustworthy. You can begin and you can continue to love at ever deepening levels. *Love* is what was given at the beginning. As it was in the beginning, is now and ever shall be. . . .

EXERCISES IN RELEVANCY
(For Individual Use)

1. *Cultural Scripting and Counterscripting*

Each person is born into one particular culture and, usually, into several sub-cultures. Each of these cultures try to mold persons into expected patterns of behavior. To get in touch with the unique cultural aspects of your script:

- Get comfortable. Relax. Think of what it was like two, four, six generations ago.
- Picture yourself living in the same place and style as your various ancestors might have lived.
- See yourself in the kinds of homes they might have had; doing their daily tasks, going to their jobs, being born and dying, being well and sick, rich and poor.
- See yourself and your ancestors immigrating to the United States, traveling by boat, by covered wagon, or in some other way, and settling down in a rural situation or in a city.
- See yourself at holiday celebrations many generations back. Also at family unhappinesses or tragedies.
- See yourself with various ancestors discussing patterns of church attendance.
- Next, use your Adult and analytically compare what you currently do, or would like to do, with what you think your ancestors did.
- Then evaluate how your cultural background has affected your script.
- Then consider whether you have any culturally determined counterscripts.
- Last, think about it. Are your script and counterscript in harmony or in conflict? What are the implications?

2. *An Individual Drama*

- Review the chapter on scripts. Try to determine what the theme of your script is. Then fill in the blanks below with cast of characters, actions, etc. (Beginning at Act III the ages in parentheses are only suggestive, they're not intended to be exact.)
- Use your imagination and guess at what your last act or acts could be *if you continue as you are now.*
  Prologue (Parental attitudes and birth experiences)

Act I (Early childhood)

Act II (Adolescence)

Act III (18–30)

Act IV (30–50)

Act V (50–70)

Act VI (70–Final Curtain)

3. *Script Check List*

Try to fill in the blanks honestly, without censoring yourself. Then go back and look over what you wrote. Make changes.

- The kinds of things that happen to me over and over again (with money, with family, with job) indicate that my script is basically:

  Constructive___ Destructive___ Going nowhere___

- It is similar to a:

  Comedy___ Tragedy___ Melodrama___ Adventure
  _____ Pilgrimage_____ Farce_____ Other_____

- The script role I play most often with people close to me is:

  Persecutor_____ Rescuer_____ Victim_____

- Most often I choose friends and expect them to play the role of _____ with me.

- What I do to attract them is: _____

- The kinds of things that happen to people like me are: _____

- The theme of my script could be summarized in the words: _____

  _____

- If an audience saw a movie of my life, from birth to today, the audience would: _____

  _____

- If the audience talked about me and my drama they would say: _____

  _____

- If I keep going the way I am now, the final curtain will come down on a scene of: _____

  _____

- When I think of this final scene I feel: _____

  _____

- The kind of audience response I want at my final curtain is: _____

- What I want people to say about me after I die is:

  _____

- The kind of heritage I want to leave my family

and friends is: _____

- To get what I want I will need to: _____

  instead of _____
  which I am now doing.

4. *Permission to Change*

Everyone lives by some of the do's and don't's heard
from their parents. Some of them have been necessary: "Don't play on a busy street," (meaning, "I care
about you, so be careful") and some may have been
unnecessarily inhibiting: "Don't you dare interrupt,"
(meaning "Nothing you could say is important") or
"Don't worry about it, I'll tell you what to do," (meaning, "I'll do your thinking for you.").

Some people resist changing, resist rebelling against
outmoded do's and don't's because they have an unrealistic fear that people won't like them if they do.
If you are like that, the following may help:

My negative do's and don't's	How they affect me now	What I could change	Fear of what will happen if I do change
_____	_____	_____	_____
_____	_____	_____	_____
_____	_____	_____	_____
_____	_____	_____	_____

- Now look at your list of what could be changed.
- Ask yourself "What is the *worst* thing that could
  happen if I change _____ and do _____
  instead of _____?"
- When you have the answer then ask the question again, "Then what is the worst thing that
  could happen?"
- Your Adult can be in control. It can protect your
  own Child and give it permission to change.

EXERCISES IN RELEVANCY
(For Group Use)

5. *Cultural Differences in Scripting*

As a warm up, ask each person to introduce themselves by their full name, including any change that might have been made in it, and to briefly describe the culture which their name reflects.

Ask participants to work on Exercise 1 for individuals (Cultural Scripting and Counterscripting) at home and jot down a few of their insights.

- In small groups (no more than five persons) let each person explain his or her cultural background.
- Then guess at how this background may affect their participation in the church.
- Others need to be encouraged to listen actively, ask questions, give feedback, but not discuss themselves while someone else is talking.

6. *Scripty Behavior*

Go into small groups and discuss how people in a church might act "scripty" on the basis of their childhood experiences and psychological positions taken in childhood.

Childhood Experiences	I'm OK, You're OK	Scripty Behavior
_____	_____	_____
_____	_____	_____
_____	_____	_____
_____	_____	_____

Childhood Experiences	I'm not-OK, You're OK	Scripty Behavior
_____	_____	_____
_____	_____	_____
_____	_____	_____

Childhood Experiences	I'm OK, You're not-OK	Scripty Behavior
_____	_____	_____
_____	_____	_____
_____	_____	_____

Childhood Experiences	I'm not-OK, You're not-OK	Scripty Behavior
_____	_____	_____
_____	_____	_____
_____	_____	_____
_____	_____	_____

7. *Drama Roles in Scripture*

- As a group, select three well-known Bible stories or parables.
- Look up the details if necessary for clarification.
- Decide if the people in the stories were playing the script roles of Rescuer, Persecutor, or Victim or not.
- If so, what did they do to get other people to play complementary roles?

• Discuss what each one of the characters could have done instead.

8. Drama Roles in the Ecumenical Movement

• Select three social action issues that are of concern to ecumenical or interfaith groups.
• Are any script roles being played by individuals or groups involved in these issues? If so, by whom?
• Why do you think so? Do you have objective Adult data? Are your Child feelings involved? Is your prejudicial Parent influencing your response?
• Select three issues on faith and order that are of concern to ecumenical or interdenominational groups.
• Are any script roles being played by individuals or groups involved in these issues? If so, by whom?
• Why do you think so? Do you have objective Adult data? Are your Child feelings involved? Is your prejudicial Parent influencing your response?
• Now reflect on how the drama roles might have been acted out in the group discussion you just had.

9. Church History Exercise

Historically, churches have been Victimized and Rescued by religious organizations and secular movements. Churches have also Persecuted other religious organizations and secular governments. They have played each of the roles in the drama triangle.

Think of the various branches of the church. Select one and fill in the blanks.

Rescuer	When?____	With whom?____	How?____
Victim	When?____	With whom?____	How?____
Persecutor	When?____	With whom?____	How?____

- Try another branch and do the same.

To predict the future of a particular church, answer and discuss the following:

- What happens to a pastor, teacher, deacon, etc. like me who _____?

- What happens to a church like ours which _____?

- What do children receive when they come to a church school like ours that _____?

10. Protection and Permission for the Child

If people are to change, they need "permission" to do so. They also need "protection" as they try out new behavior. They need this protection from someone who is psychologically strong (potent) and has an uncontaminated Adult. Therefore:

- If there is time, each person can first study the Exercise 4 for individuals (Permission to Change).
- Next, form small groups and make lists of several things in the church that need changing.
- Evaluate the arguments against change and the arguments for change.
- Decide on what "permissions" would be necessary for these changes to happen.
- Consider whether any form of "protection" would be needed during the period of change.
- Does a particular "potent" person need to give the permission and protection? If so, how can it be arranged?

11. Script Party

Parties are fun if people allow their creative, fun-loving Child to express itself. A script party can do that.

- Allow a couple of weeks for enthusiasm to build.
- Send invitations that read something like "Come as your favorite storybook character."
- Decorate the setting in a storybook way. Maybe posters, streamers, carrousel music, etc., or imitation cobwebs, spooky sounds, etc.
- When guests arrive ask each person to play out their role until others guess who they are.
- Give big gold stars for most creative costume, etc.

P.S. *Hints for Costumes*

At one script party each person in a family came dressed as a character from Little Red Riding Hood, another person wore a dress of half rags and half glamor to show herself as half princess and half Cinderella and to indicate she was rewriting her script. One man came as The Lone Ranger and his wife dressed as a horse. Their scripts fit because hers was about the horse, National Velvet.

YOU CAN
FIND MEANING
IN TIME

GETTING READY FOR A MEETING

The Budget Committee of First Church met on the last Friday evening of each month. The Committee was made up of six members plus Tom Hardy, who preferred to think of himself as a research person rather than a designated leader. On this particular Friday, each of the committee members were re-organizing their time in preparation for the meeting.

In the home of J. L. Mark, doors were slamming and children were crying. "What's going on around here?" J. L. stormed as he walked in the door, "Why can't dinner ever be ready on time?"

"Well!" snapped Karen, his wife. "Well, dinner isn't on time because you're never here on time! You've always got just one more thing to do at the office. You stop off at the bar with the boys on the way home. I'm sick and tired of trying to have meals on time for you when you're never here."

"But you know that tonight I have to be at that finance meeting at the church. Oh, why in hell, how in hell, did I ever get wrapped up in that committee?"

"Well, when they asked for committee volunteers, I volunteered you because I thought you'd be good for it. After all, you know Roberts' Rules of Order. When I suggested you for parliamentarian I thought that you'd be pleased! But I never seem to do anything right," and Karen burst into tears.

"Oh, damn it," responded J. L., "even with rules of order, nothing seems to get done. Just a bunch of yakking and yakking. What's the matter with people anyway? Why don't they shape up and settle down and get the job done?"

Meanwhile, in the Hardy home the children had left the table. Tom was eating his last bit of dessert while working intently with a yellow pad and pencil trying to outline an agenda for the evening. He realized the Budget Committee was one that had trouble getting things done. Although he had originally thought that J. L. was a good choice as chairman, being the sort of man who stuck by Roberts' Rules, Tom had come to the conclusion that J. L. slowed things down by insisting on things going in certain ways. His parental leadership hindered spontaneous interchange and creative thinking. Tom hoped that having an agenda might move things along faster.

Betty Hardy had something different going on inside of her. She was annoyed because Tom spent so many evenings away from home. Her ironing had piled up, and after she had worked in the mental health clinic that morning, the phone had rung all afternoon. Well, it seemed like all afternoon. She had forgotten to defrost the pot roast, so supper was a quick meal of creamed tuna on toast. She wished for an evening alone with Tom or maybe just the two of them going to the movies. "Meetings, meetings, meetings!" she thought to herself. "I'm sick and tired of them. There's no time for us."

Then as Tom was putting on his coat to leave, she flared up, "You take care of everybody else, and I'm stuck here alone!"

"Here we go again," thought Tom. Aloud he said, "Betty I'm really sorry. Can we talk tonight when I get home?"

Patti Browning, Church School Superintendent, was also working with paper and pencil in preparation for the evening meeting. Patti held several jobs and sometimes felt frustrated trying to do all of them well. She lived alone; her husband was dead and her children off to college. With a Master of Divinity degree and a concern for people, Patti was well equipped to be superintendent. However, as no pay was attached to the job, she had to supplement the small insurance income left by her husband in other ways. She did this by leading retreats for interdenominational groups and teaching adult education courses. She was an excellent teacher. However, Patti's air of diffidence and subservience sometimes got in her way. She was often silent on both church and denominational committees or helpful to others only by her skilled use of reflective listening. Patti was unwilling to be aggressive and acted as though she was still hiding under a table as she had when she was a little girl.

Anne Green, the teacher, had phoned Patti and asked for a ride to the meeting, a request Patti granted reluctantly because she sometimes resented Anne's "stupid" suggestions regarding budget matters and didn't know how to help Anne to respond differently.

Patti recognized Anne's assets and knew she was a good teacher. She knew that Anne felt uneasy in the presence of adults but that this did not interfere with her work in the church school. Patti also knew Anne had the kind of imagination that could create lessons that young children responded to.

Meanwhile, across town Myra was watching the clock. It was almost seven, and she was hurrying Julie and Donnie through supper because Mr. Pennyworth had asked her to come to the budget committee meeting tonight to take minutes. Inwardly Myra fumed. Rarely did she get so upset. She wished she hadn't said she would do it. Why did she say yes so often? Not only would she still have to change her clothes, but she had forgotten to put gas in the car.

Evening meetings were always inconvenient. Dick, her husband, often had to work late and the children

*needed to eat at a reasonable hour. She did not like
to leave them alone and was feeling anxious when
she heard the car door slam. She opened the door as
Dick came up the steps.*

*"Hurry," she called out as Dick came in, "I've got
to get going." Then, although she had not meant to
complain, she said "I don't see why I have to go to
that meeting tonight. Anyone on the committee can
write just as well as I can. Furthermore, I'm supposed
to quit at four. Evening meetings shouldn't be my
responsibility just because I'm church secretary."*

*Dick was not interested in church personally, so
this gave him a ready-made chance to air a long-held
resentment. "Why don't you quit that job and get a
decent one, anyway?" he grumbled. "You're not paid
enough. You only get two weeks' vacation. What's
more, I'd like to buy that boat I've been talking about.
Get rid of that dumb job and come boating with me
instead on Sunday morning. You're always running
around that church cleaning up somebody else's
messes."*

*Myra was taken aback at Dick's strong statement
about her job. She really enjoyed her job in the church
office. She liked the responsibility. It was close to
home. It was really OK.*

*When Myra left for the meeting that night, it was
with a lot of unfinished business going around in
her head.*

*"Oh, heck! Why did I blow up like that? Just when
Dick came home tired and hungry. He didn't even
kiss me when I left. I should have said 'No' to Mr.
Pennyworth. Maybe I need to plan my time more
realistically. I really believe a man and wife need to
give some of their best to each other, not just their
leftovers and their fatigue at the end of the day."*

*Ed, the custodian of First Church was also getting
ready for the meeting. He straightened the tie that
felt unfamiliar around his brawny neck and looked
at himself in the mirror. "Yes," he thought, "I'm not*

so bad looking. I work hard, too, but nobody ever notices. Well, they'll notice me tonight when I ask the committee for a raise. And boy, if I don't get it, well, they'll be sorry and they'll have a hard time getting someone to fill my spot. It'll serve them right. That's for sure!"

Lisa Rogers also dressed for the committee. Her husband traveled during the week and she had started dropping in to J. L.'s office rather frequently. Whenever Lisa went to a meeting she had the admiring eyes of numbers of men. With her beautifully applied makeup, she used her eyes lavishly to give them a come on.

One man had just resigned from the committee after getting "conned" by Lisa. She'd given him the eye on Sunday morning. He had taken it seriously and, knowing her husband was out of town, had dropped by her house. With hands on hips, Lisa humiliated him with "How dare you!" Lisa felt that such incidents were never her fault no matter how enticingly she dressed or whatever innuendos she managed to give men.

Joe Miles, getting ready in his apartment, was a little bit nervous. He was hoping that something constructive would happen in the meeting and was willing to go more than half way if it did. This was only Joe's fourth time meeting with this committee. The first time he'd gone he had come away absolutely amazed because the committee members didn't seem to know or care about each other. He couldn't believe it. Joe was actively in search of intimacy. He was still caught up in the fire of youth. He still had dreams that something real could transpire between people. Although he participated in the rituals of the church and was able to pass the time with superficial discussion on most occasions, he churned within for encounters of significance with others. All week he had been thinking carefully about this meeting. He hoped to suggest some new styles of worship that *would appeal to young people. The young people also needed some new sports equipment. "But it won't work," he said to himself as he went out the door. "Bill Pennyworth will be there and probably put down anything I say."*

At the same time, just two blocks away, Bill Penny-worth was going through the routine of cleaning up his little kitchen after a simple, lonely dinner. As he scraped a leftover potato into the garbage, Bill glanced into the other room of his tiny apartment. There, the late afternoon light reflected from the glass of the old photograph of his wife, now dead, and his two grown sons who lived many miles away. He caught their smiles.

Sighing, Bill dropped into a tattered, well-used chair. For a moment his head sank on his hands. His light blue eyes clouded with faint traces of tears but only for a moment. "What's the matter with me?" Bill thought. "I just seem to say things all wrong. People don't drop by and they never invite me out. What's the matter?"

Only briefly did Bill allow what he considered his "moment of weakness." Taking a deep breath, he picked up the church account books from the table and started out the door to walk the lonely two blocks to the meeting.

TIME STRUCTURING

Each person going to the meeting at First Church had "structured" his or her time to include this committee activity. Each brought a unique contribution of "unfinished business" to the meeting with them— their hopes, anxieties, resentments, and so forth. Each would use their time in different ways while the meeting was actually in progress.

People structure their time to avoid boredom and to achieve some form of satisfaction. According to TA theory when people are together they can use time in six different ways.

Withdrawal

Withdrawal into fantasy is one common way of structuring time whenever two or more people are together. When withdrawing, a person often rehearses in his head what he's going to say or do in a future situation, and guesses at what others will say or do. Or he relives something in the past, often what he wishes he had said or done, or what he wishes others had said or done. Or he imagines what it would be like to be somewhere else with someone else.

Some people disguise their psychological withdrawals and hide behind a book or newspaper to avoid others. To disguise her disinterest in her husband, a wife who prides herself on reading books may justify her reading because "it's educational," and criticizes her husband who prefers a newspaper, a newscast, or a sports event on T.V. Though they are physically in each other's presence, each withdraws from direct contact with the other and may, by action, communicate their desire to be left alone.

Physical withdrawal from the church is increasing. This is preceded by the psychological withdrawal many people experience if the sermon is boring, if the leadership is authoritarian or indifferent, if a committee meeting is going nowhere, or if emotional needs are not met.

Rituals

Another common way of structuring time is by engaging in rituals. Rituals are stereotyped, predictable transactions, such as "Hello." "Hello." "How are you?" "Fine." To some people the rituals of worship carry meaning, to others they are only stereotyped transactions.

A different kind of ritual occurs in many churches at the end of the service when the pastor may stand in a kind of a receiving line while the parishioners shake his hand. They say "Nice sermon!" and he says "Thank you." Or the pastor may expand the ritual to "So glad to see you." Although rituals are necessary in church and daily life, they may leave

PSYCHOLOGICAL WITHDRAWAL
IS ONE WAY TO STRUCTURE TIME

People withdraw from each other out of hurt, fear,
loneliness, or discontent. If one person withdraws from
another who wants to be involved, then both may

experience frustration. If both choose to withdraw,
each may experience a sense of detachment.

people feeling unfulfilled. If a pastor preaches a provocative sermon he has worked hard on and the parishioners ritually shake his hand and mumble "Nice sermon," the pastor will feel let down. He needs more response than a ritual offers.

Pastimes

A third way people structure their time is by pastimes, conversations at a socially acceptable level. Sports, school, cars, children, jobs, homes, and gardens are a few of the things people talk about to pass time. Pastime talking is usually *at* someone, not *to* someone. In the church, pastimes are frequent at such occasions as the coffee hours after Sunday services. They are also the desultory conversations that often take place before a meeting, after a meeting, or during a meeting.

Activities

The fourth way of structuring time is with activities with others, including work. Activities involve the manipulation of physical materials as when building a house, playing chess, buying a dress, or they involve the objective exchange of information such as, "What is that?" "It's a petunia." In activities people talk *to* each other, not *past* or *at* each other, as they do in rituals, pastimes, or games.

Activities in the church include conducting an every-member canvas, organizing a church school, and rehearsing a choir. When the custodian mows the grass in front of the church or cleans up after a wedding, or when the secretary takes a message that a parishioner is in the hospital and relays the message to the pastor, they are engaged in activities.

Games

Games arise in the midst of any of the above-mentioned ways of structuring time. For example: If one person withdraws into meditation, another may feel neglected and play *If It Weren't for Him (and his meditation practices)*. If one person offers a ritual

GREETINGS ARE RITUALS THAT USE TIME

Rituals are stereotyped predictable transactions.
A greeting such as "Hello," "Hello," is a basic two-stroke ritual in which each participant gives one
stroke of verbal recognition to the other. If they
continue with something like "How are you?" "Fine,
thank you," the transaction has four strokes. If a
person refuses to answer or gives an unpredictable
response, it usually indicates that a game is starting.

CASUAL CONVERSATION IS A PASTIME

Pastimes are similar to rituals, though not so stereotyped.
During pastimes people talk about socially acceptable
subjects. They may be hoping for a moment of intimacy
or they may be trying to avoid intimacy—or they may
be "psyching out" someone to play a game with.

ACTIVITIES BRING PEOPLE TOGETHER

A GAME IS A WASTE OF TIME

When people are working at something together
they are engaged in an activity. Whether their
work is successful is really not the point; the point
of an activity consists in people having a
common goal and working together toward it.

Games are played to collect familiar feelings,
such as depression, envy, or anger. Although it
takes only one person to start a game (by gossiping,
for example), it takes two or more to play.
Any person caught in a game can break it up.

LOVE AND JOY ARE PART OF INTIMACY

Intimacy always involves some part of the Child ego state.
Intimacy usually emerges in the midst of an activity,
when people suddenly experience a moment of
loving closeness.

"Hello," expecting a "Hello" back, another person may instead respond with a game of *Ain't It Awful* (*what's going on in the choir*). If one person starts a pastime about the church school, another might pounce on an innocuous statement with the game, *Now I've Got You, You S.O.B.* In the middle of an activity such as a budget meeting, one person may suddenly "forget" the important points and play *Stupid.* Games, as a way of transacting with people, are destructive of love.

Intimacy

This is the opposite of a game. Everyone, at the deepest level of his or her being, wants intimacy, though many shy away from it because they are afraid to trust.

Intimacy, the most precious way of experiencing time, enhances love. It cannot be structured by someone who gets up in the morning and says, "Now today I will have intimacy." It *may* happen if a person, for example, gets up in the morning and says, "Maybe today it will happen if I am alert to the possibilities." A person can anticipate intimacy but cannot force it. Intimacy happens by the grace of *Love.* It occurs in the midst of something else, usually in an activity of some sort. It is a moment of genuine dialogue without games, pastimes, rituals, or withdrawal. It is a moment filled with meaning when love enters in.

STROKING AND TIME STRUCTURING

According to Eric Berne, everyone structures their time to get "strokes."[2] A stroke is a physical touch or some symbolic form of recognition. If a child does not receive sufficient strokes, his growth—physiological, intellectual, and emotional—is impaired. Strokes are either positive or negative. Being hugged is a positive stroke; being spanked a negative one. If a child does not get *positive* strokes he or she will do something to get *negative* strokes. Strokes are so necessary for existence that children prefer negative strokes to being ignored.

As children grow older, the physical strokes they receive are partially replaced by other forms of recognition. A smile, a "hello," a handshake become substitute strokes for the hugs of infancy. A frown, a sneer, a sarcastic remark become substitute strokes for the spanking.

A ritual such as "Hello," "Hello," provides minimal recognition. It implies, "I know you're there." A handshake or peck on the cheek can do the same. Pastimes involve more transactions and therefore provide more strokes. In rituals and pastimes, as well as in shared activities, the strokes given are usually positive. They enhance a person's well-being. In intimacy the strokes given and received are pure gold strokes of love. They heal and give meaning.

Games provide negative strokes, which, tragically, is one reason people play them. Negative strokes feel better than no strokes. They also imply, "I know you're there," and that feels better than the anguished loneliness that comes from being isolated or ignored.

DIFFERENT STROKES
FOR DIFFERENT FOLKS

Many positive strokes, given with good intentions, miss the target. This is because the person giving them has *assumed* that a certain stroke would be well received instead of data processing what kind of stroke the person actually wants.

For example: If, when a little girl is sick, she is often given English muffins and applesauce by a concerned mother, she will look for that when grown. Tea and toast from a well-meaning friend (who probably was given that by her mother) will not quite hit the target.

If, when a little boy is sick, he is brought into the livingroom to talk and play with the family, he will, when grown, continue to like the involvement. If his wife goes off with the children to give him "some peace and quiet" like she had as a child, her well meaning stroke will miss its target.

Each ego state in each person may want different

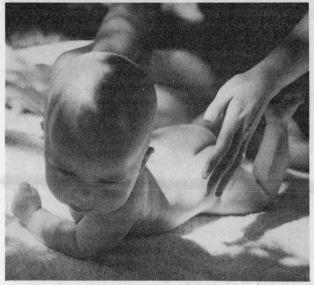

The loving touch of a mother helps a child grow physically, mentally, and emotionally. If a child is not touched enough, or is touched brutally or seductively, he or she may have severe problems later in life.

kinds of strokes. In a close relationship people can verbalize this to each other and practice giving the kinds of strokes that are desired (see Fig. 7.1).

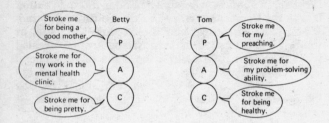

Fig. 7.1 Some of Betty and Tom Hardy's stroke needs

Traditionally, many women have been stroked for their nurturing abilities and their shapely appearance. These have been strokes to their Parent and Child ego states. However, more and more women are strengthening their Adults, are asking that the thinking ability of their Adult be recognized in church, at home, and on the job.

Traditionally, many men have been stroked for their Adult achievement, not for their nurturing abilities or appearance. However, more and more men are becoming involved in using their Parent in rearing and teaching children. They are also becoming aware of Child feelings they didn't know they had, such as the pleasure they experience when wearing bright colors and the resentment for continually being appraised because of strength, rational skills, or money-making abilities. More and more men are asking that their Parent and Child ego states also get recognition.

MEANINGFUL TIME

Among the ancient biblical people there was little concern about time as it is now generally perceived. Hours, days, months, or years were not focuses of interest to them. They placed far more importance

on the meaning of events, such as wars, reigns of
kings, births, or deaths.

When the ancient Hebrews spoke of harvest time
they weren't concerned about calendar months, rather
it was the harvest itself that made the time *meaning-
filled*. When they spoke of the exodus, the exile, or
the reign of kings it was because the *events* revealed
what has often been called "the signs of the times."
They believed that an event-filled time was an op-
portune time which called forth a response. It was
the challenge of the event, and the response it
evoked, which gave meaning to time.

The same idea of significant, meaning-filled time
was carried over into the New Testament, and the
Greek word, *kairos*, was used to distinguish it from
time measured by the clock. The well-known passage,
"The time is fulfilled," meant to New Testament
writers that the time was right for the coming of the
Messiah. In modern vernacular this is expressed as
"the timing is right."

In contrast to biblical people, modern western man
is caught up in time as measured by a clock. This is
chronological time, or *chronos*. To live by chronos,
measured time, is to live by the clock. People who do
this often check their watch or calendar. They are
more concerned with measuring the number of minutes or hours than evaluating the intrinsic meaning
of what they do. Such people speak of "wasting time,"
of "time dragging," or of "time running out." For
them time is not event-filled, therefore it has little
meaning.

The ancient concepts of chronos and kairos time
can be compared with transactional analysis categories for structuring time. Sometimes it is chronos
when people are engaged in rituals or pastimes. And
sometimes these ways of structuring time do have
some kind of meaning. A ritual "hello" and handshake, or the intonation of a well-known prayer and
response, may strike a deep chord within a person—
and when they do, it is a moment of kairos. Games,
however, usually provide negative meaning, because
someone usually feels bad when the game is com-

pleted. Psychological withdrawal often results from similar negative meaning. If a person finds a situation to be hurtful or boring he may withdraw to the safety of his own mind. Activities can be meaningless or they can be filled with meaning. When meaning-filled, they lead to intimacy and are experienced as kairos.

Each person needs to find his or her own meaning. Without this he or she may conclude that life itself is meaningless. That is a false conclusion, because every moment measured by the clock is the meaning-filled *call* to respond, to respond with the totality of our being because we were born to love.

END OF TOM'S EVENING

It was almost midnight when Tom Hardy finally closed the door of the church. He was whistling as he gingerly put his foot on the starter of his car which, at 80,000 miles, was getting a little temperamental.

Myra, Patti, and Anne had left smiling. So had Ed. Lisa's husband had come to pick her up and she had seemed generally happy to see him. J. L. Mark, with an unusually loud voice, had yelled "Cheers!" as he drove off, and there going down the street toward the ice-cream parlor were Joe Miles and Bill Pennyworth.

"Well," said Tom to himself, "it sure was different tonight. I wonder why." He recalled that instead of formally droning out, "The meeting will now come to order," J. L. had bowed his head briefly, looked up suddenly, and started with a joke circulating among the 5th graders, "Why didn't they play cards on the ark?" Anne responded, "Because Noah was sitting on the deck." She followed this with, "How did Jonah feel when the whale swallowed him?" and Joe had chortled, "Down in the mouth." Myra had beamed at the interchange. She'd have something funny to tell her children. The corners of Bill's mouth actually turned up in a smile. Maybe he was thinking of his children and what it was like when they were little.

The meeting continued to be unlike previous budget meetings. When Joe requested money for a new volleyball and net for the young people, and Ed requested a small increase in pay, Bill nodded his head in approval.

"Maybe that's when it happened," thought Tom. "When Bill said he'd raise his pledge five dollars a month when he really can't afford it, somehow that did it. It was so unexpected. Everyone picked up the challenge and pledged more, even me! Well, that was really something. Then when J. L. promised to call on five church families and ask them to give, though they never had, that made things go even better. Patti said she'd ask her father for his fine piano so it could be enjoyed in the church rather than remain in storage as it had for five years. Lisa offered to lead the cherub choir which had been leaderless for a month. Well, it was a small-sized love miracle!

"Yes," continued Tom to himself, "it was a meaning-filled evening. Like kairos time, when meaning enters in and the clock is irrelevant.

"Maybe it was because Bill decided not to veto everything. Maybe it was the joking between J. L., Anne, and Joe. Maybe it was because Lisa was more honest and not playing Rapo. Maybe it was because the Spirit seemed to be there. I wonder why? We were talking more about what people need and what we could do about it than about God and what we should do to please Him.

"Some committee members," thought Tom, "must have come to the meeting reluctantly. Still, they established a warm, emotional climate. Each one felt accepted. The activities of the committee were completed without games, rituals, pastimes, or withdrawals. The meaning-filled time had come again in a spirit of intimacy. Maybe that's what genuine dialogue is all about. Maybe that's when we meet the God in each one of us."

Ten minutes later Tom entered his house. It was quiet. Everyone must be asleep. It had been a long thirty hours since the pot-luck supper the night before.

*So much had happened. Jean Pillar's explosion, Sally's
death, the crisis with Herb and June Vague, the men's
luncheon, the evening meeting. There was so much
that still needed doing. Like seeing Bob and his family
and helping Sally's parents plan her funeral, planning
with the youth group. They had phoned and requested
a special memorial service. Maybe Joe could help
with that, and then Austin Tenor evidently was upset
and needed some time.*

Tom dropped into a big chair.

*The memory of Betty's anger during dinner re-
turned. He needed to think about it. As Tom reached
over to pick up his worn Bible, he saw a note left by
Betty, "Please wake me up when you come in. I want
to talk. June Vague phoned this evening. She said
that after talking to you she decided to enroll in the
community college. I'm sorry I was angry, Tom. I
really love you."*

*Tom woke Betty gently, but no words passed be-
tween them. They looked in each other's eyes, tenderly
put their arms around each other, and once more
experienced the love that was there in the beginning.*

A TA GOAL

Intimacy is experienced when we are who we are
and make contact openly and honestly with others
who are who they are. In intimacy there is the appreciation of differences. There is no effort to manipulate the other into some role.

Moments of intimacy happen; they can never be
forced. They occur when we respond clearly, without
guise or games, without ritual or routine, directly to
each other. This type of response is most frequently
observed in the responsible person who says "I am I"
and "I am what I am."

Intimacy usually occurs in the midst of some
activity. For example, on Sunday morning a choir
member who enjoys singing her favorite hymn may
catch the eye of a stranger, a visitor who is attending
this church on this single occasion. Suddenly they
are aware of the bond they have through mutual

enjoyment of particular words and music. A certain look passes between them. They are no longer strangers. However, this momentary intimacy may not continue. The two may never see each other again. But for that moment they were there and totally aware.

Intimacy can also occur in continuing long-term relationships. In such cases, however, the sense of intimacy is not continuous. It ebbs and flows. However, people who have known this moment await it again and again with anticipation. They recognize and respond when, by grace, it happens.

Intimacy is always game-free. It repeats the *Love* given to each one of us "in the beginning." It has a healing, reconciling quality. Any church can be a setting where this can happen. *Love* is our salvation; *Now* is the time of fulfillment; *Here*, where each of us stand, is our opportunity and challenge. If we respond, here and now, the moment will be filled with meaning, and "our cup runneth over" once again.

EXERCISES IN RELEVANCY
(For Individual Use)

1. Say Hello

The word "Hello" is usually said as part of a ritual. It gives a minimal stroke to the person who receives it. People who say "Hello" usually expect a "Hello" back. Try something new for several days.

- Say hello to people you ordinarily wouldn't speak to.
- Be aware of your Child feelings as you do so.
- Listen to your inner dialogue.
    What does your Parent say as you do this?
    How does your Child answer?
- How does each person you say "hello" to respond?

2. Time Structuring with People

Withdrawal into one's thoughts or fantasies is common when one is trying to solve a problem, create something new, or disguise feelings of boredom, anger, and so forth.

- Think about the last 24 hours.
- Recall where you went, who you saw, how you felt, and what you thought.
- Did you withdraw psychologically?
- If so, what precipitated your withdrawal?
- How did it affect the other person?
- After you withdrew, what happened next?
- Did anyone withdraw from you? If so, what was your feeling?
- What did you do?

Rituals and *pastimes* with others are useful ways of structuring time to establish an emotional climate that is usually nonthreatening to the Child ego state.

- Think about the last 24 hours.
- Recall where you went, who you saw, how you talked, and what you talked about.
- Did either the rituals or pastimes lead into games? If so, how did the game progress? How did you structure your time after the game payoff?

Games are played by everyone even though they are an unsatisfactory way of structuring time.

- Think of the last 24 hours.
- Recall where you went, who you saw, what you talked about, and how you felt.
- Were any of your feelings negative? If so, was a game being played covertly or overtly?

  Did you start it or were you "conned" into it?

  What happened when the game finished?

Activities and *intimacy* can give meaning to time. Activities without meaning are more like rituals or pastimes. They are often automatic and boring.

- Think of the last 24 hours.
- Recall where you went, who you saw, and what you did.

- If you were working around someone, were you working *together*? Or were you working as individuals though in the same place?
- How did you feel during your activities with others?
- Did feelings of intimacy emerge between you? If so, what precipitated the feelings? What happened when the period of intimacy passed?

3. *Time Structuring in a Drama*

This is to sharpen your Adult ability to observe and analyze the ways people use time.

- Watch a T.V. drama for a straight 15 minutes.
- Analyze the characters' time structuring patterns. How do the pastimes, games, etc. fit into the drama script?
- Next watch a newscast. How many of the six ways of structuring time did you observe?
- Now watch some advertisements. What forms of time structuring are shown? What is said or shown in an attempt to influence you and the way you might spend your time?

4. *Kairos and Intimacy*

Planned withdrawal into fantasy is one way of re-experiencing the healing moments of kairos.

- Get comfortable. Imagine you are watching a movie of yourself that starts when you are about 12 years old.
- Look for a scene *where you feel close to someone* (parent, teacher, pet, friend, etc.) but don't be dismayed if you don't see yourself at that age.
- Go backward in time. Look for intimacy at age 11. Age 10. Age 9. Age 8. Age 7. Age 6. Age 5. Age 4. Age 3. Age 2.
- Keep watching your movie closely. What interferes with intimacy? What is conducive to intimacy?
- Now come back to your current existence. What do you feel or do that interferes with intimacy?

What do you feel or do that is conducive to intimacy?

- Is what you currently do related to your childhood experiences? If so, how?
- Are you pleased with the *meaning* you find in your activities? If not, is there anything you can do?
- Are you pleased with the relationships of intimacy that you currently experience? If not, is there anything you can do?

EXERCISES IN RELEVANCY
(For Group Use)

5. *Hello Again*

The word "Hello" is usually part of a ritual. There are other ways to say hello.

- Push the chairs and tables out of the way.
- In silence and with eyes closed, mill around as a group for about five minutes. Be aware of how you avoid encountering people or how you reach out to find them.
- Now, still in silence and with eyes closed, find someone as a partner and get acquainted with them by touching hands. Let your hands say "Hello" to each other.
- Now touch each other's face and let your touch say "Hello."
- Now say "Hello" with your voice.

6. *Time Structuring in a Church*

Working in small groups for not more than 15 minutes, fill in the following blanks with ways people can structure their time in a church.

- Withdrawal

_____   _____

_____   _____

_____   _____

_____   _____

- **Rituals**

  _____   _____
  _____   _____
  _____   _____
  _____   _____

- **Pastimes**

  _____   _____
  _____   _____
  _____   _____
  _____   _____

- **Games**

  _____   _____
  _____   _____
  _____   _____
  _____   _____

- **Activities**

  _____   _____
  _____   _____
  _____   _____
  _____   _____

- **Intimacy**

  _____   _____
  _____   _____
  _____   _____
  _____   _____

7. *Time Structuring in Groups*

To analyze how people structure their time as they are doing it, plan ahead and have a tape recorder available and running.

- Let the group discuss some phase of T.A. theory that needs further clarification. Discuss this selected topic for 15 minutes.
- Then play back the tape to the group and let them decide how the time was structured and by whom.
- Next select one of the rituals of the church. Discuss its purpose and its effect. Play back the tape and analyze the time structuring in the group.

8. *Strengthening Adult Observation*

- Arrange to show a short film (8–12 minutes).
- Select one that shows transactions between people.
- Show the film once, then discuss the way the people in it structured their time.
- If possible, show the film again immediately for the purpose of observing it more closely.
- Discuss it again for new awareness.

9. *Time Structuring in Worship*

If group members have grown to trust each other and speak honestly about their feelings and thoughts, this discussion may be most enlightening, both to them and to the pastor. If they have not developed openness they may play a game such as *Look How Hard I'm Trying (to give the "right" answer)*.

- Everyone needs to have a copy of the Sunday bulletin.
- Ask each one to jot down in the left-hand margin how they perceived the worship hour to be structured.

- Then ask them to jot down in the right-hand
  margin how they structured their time during
  the worship.
- Discuss this in small groups.
- Does anything need to be done to give more
  meaning to the worship?
- If so, what can it be?
- Who has the capacity to do it?
- Who is willing to do it?

10. *Meaningful Activities*

- List on the blackboard the weekly activities of
  the church.
- Make a second list for the occasional activities
  of the church.
- Discuss which activities have meaning and to
  whom.
- Ask each person to give their reactions to the
  activities using the statements:

  "That activity is meaningful to me because
  _____."

  "That activity is not meaningful to me because
  _____."

8

EPILOGUE:
A
TRANSACTIONAL
THEOLOGY

For many years I have been trying to integrate a psychological system with a theological position. This chapter is being added at the request of many who know of my interest and my attempt to make this integration. Because psychology and theology are always in a state of change, this will not be the last word. Hopefully I will grow in wisdom and understanding. Therefore this chapter is an attempt to set forth in brief form that which interests me the most at this moment of my life, namely, loving and *Love*.

Historically churches have preached the gospel of love and at the same time engaged in witch hunts. Historically churches have attacked the secular world as unholy and at the same time manifested their own unholiness. Historically churches have preached damnation and at the same time stood in need of forgiveness.

On the other hand churches have also lived the gospel of love and been persecuted for it. They have been concerned over the injustices of the world and have tried to correct them. They have preached salvation and taught the way to it freely to anyone interested.

These and other negative and positive actions by churches reflect their changing social values and changing theological views. Changes inevitably happen when laymen and clergy interpret old truths in new ways. Transactional Analysis is a new and effective way to examine a theology of relationships. For example, because each person's ego states are different, each may have different beliefs about the use of prayer and the sacraments, the nature of God and the Church, the doctrine of sin, and the manner in which forgiveness and reconciliation takes place.

TA AND THEOLOGICAL THINKING

In some church groups traditional modes of thought are valued, in others, new ideas predominate, still others fluctuate between the two extremes. Yet any church group can analyze their agreements and disagreements by asking themselves structural analysis questions related to their ego states, such as: "What did my parent figures say or do in relation to a specific theological belief," i.e., "As a child, what was I *taught* in relation to this belief?" "How did I feel then in response to the teaching?" "What facts do I have about the validity of my parents' belief?"

Similar questions can be designed for discussions on the nature of faith. Questions such as: "What does living by faith mean?" "In which ego state does my faith seem to be?" "Do I act my faith as an Adult, feel my faith as a Child, impose my faith on others as a Parent?"

A thoughtful study group can also draw ego state portraits of their church, its governing board, and the congregation as a whole. This could be followed by analysis of the various types of transactions—complementary, crossed or ulterior—that occur when a particular belief is discussed. Questions could be designed for this, such as: "What kind of response does my faith elicit from others?" "Does my faith express love?" "Does the love reflect responsibility?" "Does healing take place in my transactions with others?"

People in the church can also analyze their individual games with questions such as: "What kind of games am I involved in at church?" "What is my payoff?" "Do I collect guilt stamps if not perfect?" "Hurt stamps if sometimes ignored?" "Depression stamps when sometimes criticized?" "Self-righteous stamps when counting up my 'good works'?" "What game do I set in motion to get these feelings?" For example, "Do I favor particular traditions or doctrines and ignore others?" If so, "Do I collect a stamp when these things are discussed?"

A study group can also analyze the games a church plays as an institution: the ways it tries to rescue (legitimately when people need it, illegitimately when people want to stand on their own feet and make their own decisions), the ways it tries to persecute (legitimately when injustices are being perpetrated, illegitimately when contributing to a guilt complex), the ways it feels victimized (legitimately when persecuted by other institutions, illegitimately when feeling bad about not having its previous high status in society).

People can also analyze their individual script in the church by asking similar questions: "What role do I most often experience around the church?" "Do I feel like someone is victimizing me?" "Do I feel that I need to continually rescue others?" "Do I feel that I would like to persecute those who disagree with me?" "What keeps happening to me over and over again in my church relations?"

Study groups can also analyze a local church script by asking existential questions such as: "If we go on as we are, what will happen in the next act?" "What will be the 'audience response' to our drama?" "Will we be satisfied with it?" "If not, how can our script be rewritten?" "What do we want, in this act and the next, that could guide the dialogue and action." "Who is the director?" "If God, then how do we know what is wanted in the next scene?" "If it is not God, then who is it?"

Many people today, both lay and clergy, revolt against the parental authoritarianism historically manifested in the churches. Yet each person reaches for a truth he can live by. If any church *insists* its tradition is the only right one, some members may comply but others are likely to rebel and search elsewhere for truth and love.

LIVING IN LOVE

To live in the *Love* that was given in the beginning
is to believe in rainbows, and the promise given that
mankind will not be destroyed. To live in love is to
enter into dialogic encounter with other peoples and
all of existence. To live in love is to experience personal wholeness and integrity. To live in love is to
trust the eternal Spirit, to listen when it speaks, to
act when it calls, which is every minute of every day.
To live in love is to be awestruck by the wonder of
how it all is interrelated—oceans crashing on the
shore, yellow mustard fields blooming after the first
spring rain, wind moaning through giant pines, a
dog barking loudly to protect its master, the eyes of
the sick, hurt, and lonely pleading for acceptance, the
innocence of an infant reaching out in trust and the
tenderness of a hand responding with "I love you."

Living in love is difficult or impossible for encapsulated people (Fig. 8.1). Such people refuse to give
of themselves and refuse to let others in. Their responses to themselves and others is conditional and
measured.

Living in love is a life style for those who are
dialogically oriented. Such people are open and vulnerable. They respond with their minds, their bodies,
and their spiritual selves. Other people are important
to them and so is the world in which they live.
Dialogic people are self-revealing. Their essence
shows through.

Martin Buber, theologian-philosopher, claims there
are two kinds of people—image people and essence
people. Image people are primarily concerned with
the impression they make on others. Image people
are like overly adapted children. They continually
wonder what others are thinking of them. Essence
people, in contrast, simply give of themselves, knowing that their basic responsibility is to respond. Their
external personality boundaries are permeable, so
they move in dialogic encounter with all the spheres
of existence.

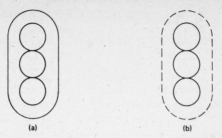

Fig. 8.1 Encapsulated vs. dialogic people.
Encapsulated people (a) wear rigid armor to keep
themselves in and others out. Dialogic people
(b) are open and transparent. They believe
in self-disclosure and accept disclosures of others.

ENCAPSULATED PEOPLE

In many relations, one or both persons are encapsulated. They are shut off from each other because
of fear, guilt, resentment, or disinterest, or because
they were adapted in childhood to "keep their distance." Encapsulated people may be high in achievement, but they are low in loving ability.

In a marriage or any other relationship, if one or
both are encapsulated because of their childhood
training or traumatic experiences, they erect psychological walls which say "Stay away," or "Leave me
alone," or "Don't get too close."

In a marriage or any other relationship, if one or
both are encapsulated because of fear, the fear may
be realistic and the armor necessary to avoid being
brutalized, physically or verbally, or the fear may be
unrealistic and a carry-over from childhood experiences. A little girl with a loud and abusive father is
likely to experience fear later in life if her husband
speaks loudly, even though he is not abusive. This
fear is unrealistic and is a carry-over from the past.

In a marriage, or any other relationship, if one or
both are encapsulated because of resentment, the

resentment may be justified, but being encapsulated is not. Many a person expects their spouse to be a mind reader of their needs and desires and are offended if the reading is inaccurate. Many a person harbors resentments for small slights when such things would be dismissed if the relationship was vital.

In a marriage, or any other relationship, if one or both are encapsulated because of disinterest, they are also critical of something about the other—appearance, intelligence, personality, etc.—and perhaps have found someone else more exciting. But people are not boring. Beneath the armor, the layers of phoniness, and the psychological games which are played out of habit or delusional self-protection, is the person who was born *to* love and *for* love.

Lovingness can be called forth. Psychological walls can melt away in redeeming dialogic encounters. But to pierce the armor of an encapsulated person is difficult. The psychological thickness of the external personality boundary may be so thick that it is permeable only during a crisis. It may be so thick that others, or the person himself, may give up trying to get through it.

MONOLOGIC RELATIONS

Although encapsulated people may talk to others, they avoid direct encounter and engage in monologue which is disguised as dialogue.

Dialogue is the open give and take of information, ideas, and even dreams. It is "from one open-hearted person to another open-hearted person."[1] When people are in dialogue they understand each other and are also understood.

Monologue may sound like dialogue because each takes turns speaking, but actually each person is talking to himself (Fig. 8.2). His words bounce back to him from the shell of his armor or from the armor of someone else. The monologic person uses others as backboards against which to throw his ideas and cares little about the other's genuine response. He wants to be feared or admired. He is concerned with his image and withholds his essence. A torturous inner conversation, usually between his Parent and his Child, occupies much of his time.

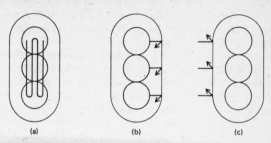

(a) (b) (c)

Fig. 8.2 The encapsulated monologic person.
(a) Inner conversations go on and on.
(b) Messages *to* others do not get through.
(c) Messages *from* others do not get through.

When talking to others, the encapsulated person is so preoccupied with what he wants to say that his message does not get through. He does not "experience the other side," meaning he doesn't see it or hear it from the other person's perspective. He uses his listener like an "it," like an object, and the relation is I-It rather than I-Thou.

The basic action of the monologic person is reflection, the bending back or refusal to accept, with one's essential being, the other person in all of his or her uniqueness. The monologic relation is expressed in four different ways:

1. When thoughts are pointedly expressed to strike home sharply without consideration of the other as a person.
2. When each person talks without purpose except to feel confirmed by making some kind of impression.
3. When each considers his own opinions to be right and the opinions of others to be questionable.
4. When each talks about his own glorious experiences without encountering or caring about the other.

FORMS OF DIALOGUE

The basic attitude of the dialogic person is fully turning to the other with body, mind, and essence. When in dialogue, people *look at* each other, *talk to* each other, not at or past each other. They do not close their eyes or look at the ceiling or floor when talking. These are signs of inner monologue. Rather they look directly at the other and speak directly to the other without evading or diluting the issue. They listen, really listen, instead of planning what they are going to say when the other person stops talking.

Dialogue takes one of two forms—technical dialogue or genuine dialogue. Technical dialogue is the exchange of information. Usually it is an Adult-Adult transaction, crisp and uncontaminated by Parent or Child. Technical dialogue results in objective understanding. In the midst of technical dialogue, genuine dialogue may spring into being. The process is similar to intimacy happening in the midst of an activity. Genuine dialogue may even occur during a silence, not just in the tender glances between lovers or a shared mystical silence, but also when the spell over an encapsulated person, who was spellbound in childhood, is lifted and his essence shines through.

The intent in genuine dialogue is to establish a living mutual relationship. This is not an intellectual activity. "There are no gifted or ungifted here, only those who give themselves and those who withhold themselves."[2] In the moments of dialogue each has in mind the other person, is "all there" with the other person, is not thinking of something or someone else, nor fantasizing that the other is different than he actually is.

DIALOGIC RELATIONS

In dialogic relations a person gives of himself, gives of his essence to the situation. To give oneself does not mean to lose one's own concreteness or identity, to get lost or swallowed up in the problems, dreams, or activities of someone else. To give oneself means to extend one's concreteness and this requires: some kind of relationship between two people, an event they experience in common, and one person, without forfeiting his own identity—or reality—living through the "common event from the stand-point of the other."[3]

If one forfeits his own reality, as often happens in an infatuation, the relationship is symbiotic rather than dialogic (Fig. 8.3).

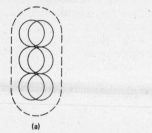 

(a)   (b)

Fig. 8.3 Symbiotic vs. dialogic relations.
(a) In a nondialogic symbiotic relation, a person's
uniqueness is lost in over-identification with
the other. (b) In a dialogic relation, one person
(or both) experience an event as the other person
experiences it, but without losing uniqueness.

Some people refuse to encounter others with the totality of themselves. They may allow one ego state to be expressed and close off the others. In such a case their dialogue, whether technical or genuine, will be very limited. Like a person who is constantly Adult, constantly Parent, or constantly Child, they repress parts of their personality (Fig. 8.4). In a marriage, for example, if one or both persons have a script theme of "Life is serious. We are here to work, not play," the Child will be encapsulated and the marriage will lack a sense of fun. Or if their script calls for a particular Parent-Child relation, e.g., "You be the little girl (boy) and I'll be the big daddy (mama)," the Adult may be shut off.

To really live is to really meet, really encounter others in genuine dialogic relations. This is not easy. The demands are considerable. They include: mutual claims, sacrifices, promises, and risks. The *claim*

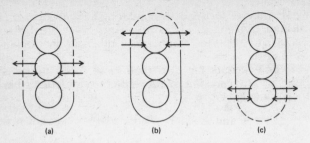

Fig. 8.4 Partially encapsulated persons. (a) Only the Adult is open to dialogue. (b) Only the Parent expresses itself freely. (c) Only the Child is open for encounter.

is for complete and vital engagement with the other. The *sacrifice* means a letting go of other possibilities because a mutual relationship demands a kind of exclusiveness at that particular moment. The *promise*, which can be spoken or unspoken, binds one to the other. The *risk* is to be vulnerable, is to give oneself wholly to someone else. The characteristic attitude and word for this kind of relation is I-Thou, and into every individual I-Thou encounter, the Eternal Thou enters in. Yet, even in the most significant relations, people move back and forth in I-Thou and I-It attitudes. It is impossible to live continually in the I-Thou. The world of everyday activities requires objective relating. However, the person who lives exclusively in the world of I-It does not really live.

The demands of a dialogic relation are difficult but they are possible because the essence is love. The life of dialogue is "not one in which you have much to do with men, but one in which you really have to do with those with whom you have to do."[4]

SPHERES OF DIALOGUE

People can establish dialogic relations in any or all of the four dialogic spheres. According to Martin Buber, *the first dialogic sphere* is "from stones to stars." Is there anyone who has not found meaning when encountering a golden sunrise or glowing sunset, a field of mustard or a desert of sand, the crash of waves or the quick movement of a small stream, a storm-tossed cypress, or a weeping willow? The writer of the eighth psalm experienced this sphere. Perhaps he walked out one night, looked up at the stars, meditated on the meaning of existence, and encountered the Eternal Thou. His words reflect the dialogue:

When I look at thy heavens, the work of thy fingers, the moon and the stars which thou hast established;

what is man that thou are mindful of him, and the son of man that thou dost care for him?

Yet thou hast made him little less than God, and dost crown him with glory and honor.

The second dialogic sphere is less commonly experienced. It is with animals and is known by those people who "have deep down in their being a potential partnership with animals—most often persons who are by no means 'animalistic' by nature, but rather spiritual."[5] In this dialogic relation a person leads an animal into his personal sphere. If the person is not phony, if he is not *pretending* to be interested but really is, the animal may respond from the whole of his being.

The third dialogic sphere is that of a "spirit" which has entered the world and can be perceived by the senses or, though hidden in the present, can unfold dialogically. The spirit is always revealed in some form. In a piece of art, a piece of practical carpentry, a tasteful dinner, or a bit of poetry, the spirit of the person creating it shows through. When I first read Martin Buber's writings some years ago, I met Buber's spirit through his writing. This same encounter happens when I read or recall certain passages in the Bible. If when I read, I "listen" as though the speaker is in my presence, I cannot treat the Bible objectively. The spirit of the original speaker encounters me in dialogue. The works confront me and demand of me a response.

Outside my bedroom window is a trellis which years ago must have held up some grape vines. It is a simple square design of two-by-fours painted white,

A tree can be scientifically
analyzed—or it can be
dialogically experienced in
an I-Thou relationship.

In dialogue each enters the
sphere of the other.

THE SPIRIT OF A PERSON SHOWS
THROUGH HIS ACHIEVEMENTS

When one enters dialogue
through experiencing
the achievements of other
people ("getting the feel"
of a bridge, for example),
the eternal Thou enters in.

plain carpentry with no artistic value *except* when
the moon cuts a geometric shadow design across the
square. Then I meet the spirit of the carpenter, and
the Eternal Thou enters into the dialogue.

The fourth dialogic sphere is that which can exist
between two or more people. The dialogue may be
onesided or fully reciprocal. For example, between a
student and his teacher, or a patient and his therapist it is onesided, because the focus is on the student
or patient who does not have a reciprocal concern for
the teacher or therapist. In this onesided relationship
the teacher or therapist tries to imagine what the
other person is "at this very moment wishing, feeling, perceiving, thinking, and not as a detached
content, but in his very reality."[6] When this happens,
the other person feels accepted, affirmed, and confirmed.

If the relationship changes and the student or
patient "imagines the real" of the teacher or therapist,
and experiences the teacher or therapist at this level
of reality, then the relationship between them may
change to one of friendship.[7] Each experiences mutual affirmation in a reciprocal dialogue.

DIALOGIC COMMUNITY

When people are in a dialogic relationship to each
other they stand together as a "we." The sense of
weness may be a temporary experience such as may
occur when a tragedy brings people together, or the
"we" may be constant as in some churches where a
few or many are committed to an I-Thou relation
with each other and strive daily to live their faith as
part of a holy community.

It is the sense of "we" that leads to the sense of
community. Community is not just a group of individuals bundled together and perhaps moving toward
one goal. No. Although community may include this,
it also includes a dialogic turning toward each other,
a breaking through of encapsulating armor and an
experiencing of each other's worlds. Community is
not a goal to be directly sought; it is a result of
people having a common goal in relation to the Eternal

Thou, the *Love* that was there in the beginning. Marriage is sometimes a dialogic community, sometimes not. So is a church. Community is where community happens.

The essence of community is love. Love is an ethical responsibility of an I for Thou. It is unconditional good will. It is wanting the best for the other without thought of return. Responsibility means responding to the claim of each moment out of the depths of being. This involves a *decision* to respond directly.

Decisionlessness, for Buber, is a failure to direct one's inner power and therefore is the essence of evil.[8] Decisionlessness is due to anxiety or fear in the Child ego state of not doing things perfectly. This feeling contaminates the Adult. Yet love requires an open-eyed trust in the world and its people, including oneself; a trust that all is of value and redeemable, that each can turn from futile decisionlessness and take the direction toward God. The direction is the heart of a community.

THE SPIRITUAL SELF

Dialogic relation is possible because of the spiritual self that is inherent in all people. We are God's Thou and our spiritual self is at the deepest core of our being.

On a principle similar to that of a percolator coffee pot, the spiritual self bubbles up and transforms the personality. Because each ego state is useful and necessary, the core of being—which is the loving spiritual self—can permeate all ego states, the entire person, body, and mind.

If the spiritual self permeates a person's Child, that person will express positive childlike qualities such as affection, warmth, curiosity, and a playfulness. If the spiritual self permeates the Adult, a person will make decisions on the basis of facts, but also on the basis of other people's feelings and well-being, and with an awareness that many decisions need to be made to preserve the total environment rather than exploit it. If the spiritual self permeates the Parent,

A common experience
or a common goal leads
to a sense of community.

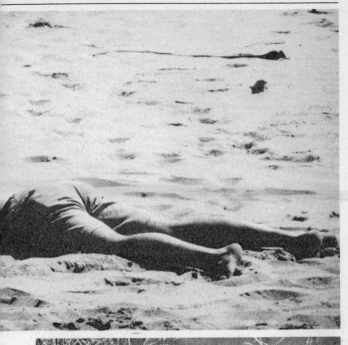

a person will express only those nurturing and positive caring qualities that can be found in parents and will not express Parent behavior that is destructive to self or others.

All ego states can be transformed when a person chooses to experience his or her spiritual self. Like the cup that runneth over love can first percolate throughout a person, then pour over toward others (Fig. 8.5).

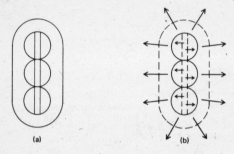

(a)   (b)

Fig. 8.5 The spiritual self. The closed-off spiritual self (a) may act ethically, yet withhold warmth and love. The open-up spiritual self (b) sends off positive vibrations of healing love. Love percolates within.

It is because we have a spiritual self that we can enter into I-Thou relations, and the spiritual self needs to be used or it becomes closed off and atrophied. When it is used, people act with *loving kindness* in spite of everything. Although it may not be possible to love everyone, it *is* possible to show loving-kindness to all people, especially if one is in touch with the spiritual self, which in turn is open to the loving God.

People who hold on to old resentments or outdated fears, who wallow in a sense of guilt, who experience themselves or the world as evil or as without value, send out negative "vibrations" that pollute or destroy themselves or others. Such people have forgotten, or never knew, that in the beginning *Love* created people —and that creation was good.

Negative feelings can be changed by conscious, deliberate, voluntary contact with your spiritual self and with the spiritual core of others. It may not be easy to get in touch with your spiritual self if you have been out of touch and alienated. Yet only you can do it and no one can do it for you.

The first step must be a genuine desire to reach out to all the spiritual forces that can be met in the four spheres of dialogue. It may seem strange if you are accustomed to busyness, to physical achievement, and to intellectual efforts. This requires more than intelligence. It requires awareness, right here, right now. Stop now as you read. Become aware, for example, of that piece of rock nearby, the fleck of dust on the glass, the feel of sun on your skin. Don't think, don't study, don't analyze. Just let your physical environment come into your consciousness. Open all your ego states to wider influences and allow for spiritual contact with each sphere of dialogue.

The practice of physical relaxation so that even the tension in the small muscles drains away is an aid to getting in touch with the spiritual self. When lying on the floor or sitting in a comfortable place, you can turn off your intellectualizing and be open to yourself and your environment. You can sense the love that you knew in the beginning to be like a percolator within. You can allow this percolating love to send out positive vibrations of love and healing.

The second step must be a genuine desire to get in touch with all the spiritual forces within you. It may be hard to believe you have a spiritual self that is a reflection of eternal love. Yet this belief is a necessity. Continuing awareness of this core of being leads to a feeling of strength, joy, and forgiveness, and conversely allows you to express your strength, joy, and forgiveness toward others as well as toward yourself. In prayer you reach toward God; in meditation God reaches toward you. Both are necessary if you are to get in touch with the spiritual self within.

During the Reformation, Martin Luther wrote that all of life is a crossing of the Red Sea. This means that coming out of slavery is assuming responsibility for who we are and what we do. This is a life-long

process that never ends. Yet *Love* directs us to take
a dialogic stand toward all of existence. This is the
beginning, because when we turn and go forth to
meet *Love*, we discover *Love* has already come to
meet us—and this is our salvation. We are chosen
and we can choose.

All the world calls us to innumerable communions,
calls us to respond out of the depths of our being,
calls us because we were born to *Love*. Each of us
also calls each other to innumerable communions,
calls each other to respond out of the depths of being,
calls each other because we were born to *be* and born
to be loving.

As it was in the beginning

Is now and ever shall be

World without end

Amen Amen

Love

FOOTNOTES
AND
REFERENCES

CHAPTER 1

1. For further information on books and journals published on Transactional Analysis write: International Transactional Analysis Association, 2155 College Ave., Berkeley, Ca. 94705.
2. Pitirim A. Sorokin, *The Ways and Power of Love*, Chicago, Henry Regnery, 1967, pp. 15–35.

CHAPTER 2

1. Eric Berne, *Games People Play*, New York, Grove Press, 1964, p. 23.
2. Muriel James, "The Use of Structural Analysis in Pastoral Counseling," *Pastoral Psychology*, 19, 187 (October 1968) pp. 8–15.

CHAPTER 3

1. Eric Berne, *Transactional Analysis in Psychotherapy*, New York, Grove Press, 1961, p. 32.
2. Muriel James and Dorothy Jongeward, *Born to Win, Transactional Analysis with Gestalt Experiments*, Reading, Mass., Addison-Wesley, 1971, p. 17.
3. *Ibid.*, p. 218.
4. *Ibid.*, p. 221.
5. Muriel James, "The Downscripting of Women for 115 Generations: A Historical Kaleidoscope," *Transactional Analysis Journal* (October 1973).
6. James and Jongeward, *ibid.*, p. 245.
7. Thanks to Robert Hoffman for this basic idea.

CHAPTER 4

1. Berne, *Games People Play*, p. 30.
2. Eric Berne, *What Do You Say After You Say Hello?*, New York, Grove Press, 1972, p. 95.
3. Eric Berne, "Standard Nomenclature, Transactional Nomenclature," *Transactional Analysis Bulletin*, 8, No. 32 (October 1969) p. 112.
4. Cf. Franklin Ernst, "The OK Corral—Grid for Get on With," *Transactional Analysis Journal* (October 1971).

CHAPTER 5

1. Berne, *What Do You Say After You Say Hello?*, p. 24.
2. Cf. Stephen Karpman, "Fairy Tales and Script Drama Analysis," *Transactional Analysis Bulletin*, 7, No. 26, (April 1968) pp. 39–43.
3. Dorothy Jongeward and Muriel James, *Winning With People: Group Exercises in Transactional Analysis*, Reading, Mass., Addison-Wesley, 1972.

CHAPTER 6

1. Berne, *What Do You Say After You Say Hello?*, p. 95.
2. *Ibid.*, p. 446.
3. *Ibid.*, p. 447.
4. Richard E. Chartier, "A Plan for Getting T.A. into Church and Community," *Transactional Analysis Bulletin*, 9, No. 33 (January 1970) p. 16.
5. Berne, *ibid.*, pp. 244–245.
6. *Ibid.*, p. 224.
7. *Ibid.*, p. 59.
8. James and Jongeward, *Born to Win*, pp. 80–81.

CHAPTER 7

1. James and Jongeward, *Born to Win*, pp. 52–59.
2. Berne, *Games People Play*, p. 15.

CHAPTER 8

1. Martin Buber, *Between Man and Man*, Boston, Beacon Press, 1955, p. 7.

2. *Ibid.*, p. 35.
3. *Ibid.*, p. 97.
4. *Ibid.*, p. 20.
5. Buber, *I and Thou*, New York, Charles Scribner's Sons, 1958, p. 172.
6. Buber, *The Knowledge of Man*, New York, Harper and Row, 1958, p. 70.
7. Buber, *Between Man and Man*, p. 101.
8. Maurice S. Friedman, *Martin Buber: The Life of Dialogue*, Chicago, University of Chicago Press, 1955, p. 32.

ABOUT THE AUTHOR

The Rev. Dr. MURIEL JAMES is author of *What to Do With Them Now That You've Got Them: Transactional Analysis for Moms and Dads* and co-author with Dorothy Jongeward of *Born to Win: Transactional Analysis With Gestalt Experiments, Winning With People: Group Exercises in Transactional Analysis,* and a new student textbook, *The People Book.* She is clinical director of the Transactional Analysis Institute, Lafayette, California. An ordained minister of the United Church of Christ, The Rev. James has her M. Div. from Church Divinity School of the Pacific (Episcopal), and has served on the visiting faculty at Pacific School of Religion (Interdenominational) and San Francisco Theological Seminary in San Anselmo (Presbyterian). Muriel James received her doctorate in the psychology of adult education from University of California, Berkeley, and is a licensed marriage and family counselor. She has served on the extension faculties of the University of California and California School of Professional Psychology. She is also vice president of the International Transactional Analysis Association.

Introducing
BANTAM NEW AGE BOOKS

This important new imprint—to include books in a variety of fields and disciplines—will deal with the search for meaning, growth and change. They are special, seminal, definitive works on subjects ranging from Eastern thought and religion to new physics, consciousness, philosophy, psychology and ecology. BANTAM NEW AGE BOOKS will form connecting patterns to help understand this search as well as mankind's options and models for tomorrow. They are books that circumscribe our times and our future. Here are the first six titles:

THE MEDUSA AND THE SNAIL by Lewis Thomas
This bestseller takes up where Thomas' THE LIVES OF A CELL leaves off. It is a collection of brilliant essays, with witty and insightful observations on the eternal issues of life and death, disease and natural death, cloning, war, and the human genius for making mistakes and much more.

LIFETIDE by Lyall Watson
Beginning with the very seeds of life and ending with a practical explanation of paranormal phenomena within nature, this ambitious work covers the biology of the unconscious, the universe, its beginnings and man's place in it. Watson is the author of SUPERNATURE and GIFTS OF UNKNOWN THINGS.

MIND AND NATURE: A NECESSARY UNITY
by Gregory Bateson

His theory is staggering: The mental system that governs how we think and learn is the same sort of system that governs the evolution and ecology of all life on earth; that man's thought processes are at times antiquated, at times paradoxical and ultimately contrary to the natural order of things.

THE DANCING WU LI MASTERS by Gary Zukav

A superb introduction to the most brilliant minds of our century including Max Planck, Albert Einstein, Neils Bohr and J.S. Bell. Zukav explains their fascinating discoveries in understandable laymen's language. *The New York Times* calls the book "the most exciting intellectual adventure since ZEN AND THE ART OF MOTORCYCLE MAINTENANCE."

TOWARD A HISTORY OF NEEDS by Ivan Illich

A seminal work by the important modern social critic and philosopher in which he squarely faces the concerns with energy and the quality of life. The book includes "Energy and Equity," the famous essay that not only predicted the energy crisis but which remains today the most influential work in the field.

MAGICAL CHILD by Joseph Chilton Pearce

The renowned author of THE CRACK IN THE COSMIC EGG explains and shows how to recover the astounding capacity we humans have for creative intelligence. A popular and controversial book on birthing and childrearing.

ALL BANTAM NEW AGE BOOKS will be
available wherever paperbacks are sold.

Heartwarming Books
of
Faith and Inspiration

☐	14725	**PILGRIMS REGRESS** C. S. Lewis	$2.50
☐	20464	**LOVE AND LIVING** Thomas Merton	$3.50
☐	20618	**A SEVERE MERCY** Sheldon Vanauken	$2.95
☐	01184	**HE WAS ONE OF US: THE LIFE OF JESUS OF NAZARETH** Rien Poortvliet	$9.95
☐	14826	**POSITIVE PRAYERS FOR POWER-FILLED LIVING** Robert H. Schuller	$2.25
☐	20133	**REACH OUT FOR A NEW LIFE** Robert H. Schuller	$2.50
☐	14732	**HOW CAN I FIND YOU, GOD?** Marjorie Holmes	$2.50
☐	13588	**IN SEARCH OF HISTORIC JESUS** Lee Roddy & Charles E. Sellier, Jr.	$2.25
☐	13890	**THE FINDING OF JASPER HOLT** Grace Livingston Hill	$1.75
☐	14385	**THE BIBLE AS HISTORY** Werner Keller	$3.50
☐	20613	**THE GREATEST SALESMAN IN THE WORLD** Og Mandino	$2.50
☐	14216	**THE GREATEST SALESMAN IN THE WORLD** Og Mandino	$2.25
☐	14971	**I'VE GOT TO TALK TO SOMEBODY, GOD** Marjorie Holmes	$2.50
☐	12853	**THE GIFT OF INNER HEALING** Ruth Carter Stapleton	$1.95
☐	12444	**BORN AGAIN** Charles Colson	$2.50
☐	14840	**A GRIEF OBSERVED** C. S. Lewis	$2.50
☐	14770	**TWO FROM GALILEE** Marjorie Holmes	$2.50
☐	20727	**LIGHTHOUSE** Eugenia Price	$2.95
☐	14406	**NEW MOON RISING** Eugenia Price	$2.50
☐	20272	**THE LATE GREAT PLANET EARTH** Hal Lindsey	$2.75

Buy them at your local bookstore or use this handy coupon for ordering:

Bantam
On Psychology

☐ 20138	**PASSAGES: Predictable Crises of Adult Life,** Gail Sheehy	$3.95
☐ 20336	**PEACE FROM NERVOUS SUFFERING,** Claire Weekes	$2.75
☐ 20540	**THE GESTALT APPROACH & EYE WITNESS TO THERAPY,** Fritz Perls	$3.50
☐ 20220	**THE BOOK OF HOPE,** DeRosis & Pellegrino	$3.95
☐ 20315	**THE PSYCHOLOGY OF SELF-ESTEEM: A New Concept of Man's Psychological Nature,** Nathaniel Branden	$3.50
☐ 14936	**WHAT DO YOU SAY AFTER YOU SAY HELLO?** Eric Berne, M.D.	$3.50
☐ 14201	**GESTALT THERAPY VERBATIM,** Fritz Perls	$2.75
☐ 14480	**PSYCHO-CYBERNETICS AND SELF-FULFILLMENT,** Maxwell Maltz, M.D.	$2.75
☐ 13518	**THE FIFTY-MINUTE HOUR,** Robert Lindner	$2.25
☐ 14827	**THE DISOWNED SELF,** Nathaniel Branden	$2.95
☐ 14940	**CUTTING LOOSE: An Adult Guide for Coming to Terms With Your Parents,** Howard Halpern	$2.75
☐ 14372	**BEYOND FREEDOM AND DIGNITY,** B. F. Skinner	$3.50
☐ 20066	**WHEN I SAY NO, I FEEL GUILTY,** Manuel Smith	$3.50
☐ 20253	**IN AND OUT THE GARBAGE PAIL,** Fritz Perls	$2.95

Buy them at your local bookstore or use this handy coupon for ordering: